WILDLIFE WATCHING

GREAT SMOKY MOUNTAINS

NATIONAL PARK

By Mike Carlton
Photography by John Netherton

NORTHWORD

NORTHWORD PRESS, INC.
Minocqua, Wisconsin

For my loving wife, Karen;
our daughters, Meaghan and Kirsten;
and my parents Bob and Jearl.

The author gratefully acknowledges the support and assistance of the staff of the U.S. Fish and Wildlife Service including Jamie Rappaport Clark, Jim Clark, Gary Henry, Chris Lucash and Barron Crawford; the National Park Service staff including Don Dafoe, John Weller and the helpful ranger staff of the Great Smoky Mountains National Park; Pete Wyatt of the Tennessee Wildlife Resources Agency; David Withers of the Tennessee Department of Environment and Conservation Natural Heritage Program and the patient editorial direction of Karen Reband-Carlton.

© Mike Carlton, 1996
Photography © John Netherton, 1996
Additional photography © 1996: Dembinsky Photo Associates: Dominique Braud, 37; Adam Jones, 58-59; Randall Henne, 93. DRK Photo: Gary Zahm, 45. The Wildlife Collection: Robert Lankinen, 64-65; Henry Holdsworth, 72; Tom Vezo, 90. Adam Jones, 91.

Cover design and map by Kenneth A. Hey
Book design by Amy J. Monday

NorthWord Press, Inc.
P.O. Box 1360
Minocqua, WI 54548

For a free catalog describing our audio products, nature books and calendars, call 1-800-356-4465, or write Consumer Inquiries, NorthWord Press, Inc., P.O. Box 1360, Minocqua, Wisconsin 54548.

Printed in Hong Kong

Library of Congress Cataloging-in-Publication Data

Carlton, Mike
    Great Smoky Mountains National Park : a wildlife watcher's guide /
by Mike Carlton ; photography by John Netherton.
        p.   cm.
    Includes bibliographical references.
    ISBN 1-55971-544-8
        1. Zoology—Great Smoky Mountains National Park (N.C. and Tenn.)
    2. Wildlife watching—Great Smoky Mountains National Park (N.C. and
Tenn.) I. Netherton, John.   II. Title
QL196.C37 1996
591.9768'89—dc20   95-24502

Contents

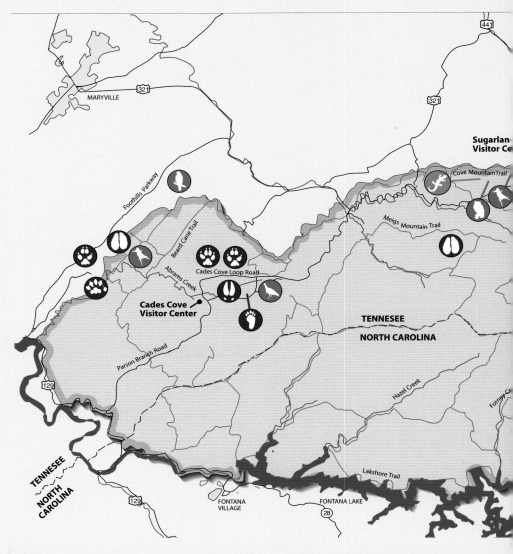

MARYVILLE

321

441

321

Sugarlan
Visitor Ce

Cove Mountain Trail

Foothills Parkway

Meigs Mountain Trail

Beard Cane Trail

Cades Cove Loop Road

Abrams Creek

Cades Cove
Visitor Center

TENNESSEE
NORTH CAROLINA

Parson Branch Road

129

Hazel Creek

Forney C

Lakeshore Trail

TENNESEE
NORTH
CAROLINA

129

FONTANA
VILLAGE

FONTANA LAKE

28

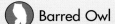 Barred Owl

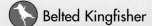 Belted Kingfisher

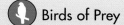 Birds of Prey

Black Bear

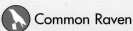 Common Raven

 Coyote

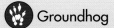 Groundhog

Long-tailed
Salamander

 Opossum

 Raccoon

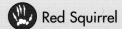 Red Squirrel

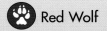 Red Wolf

GREAT SMOKY MOUNTAINS NATIONAL PARK

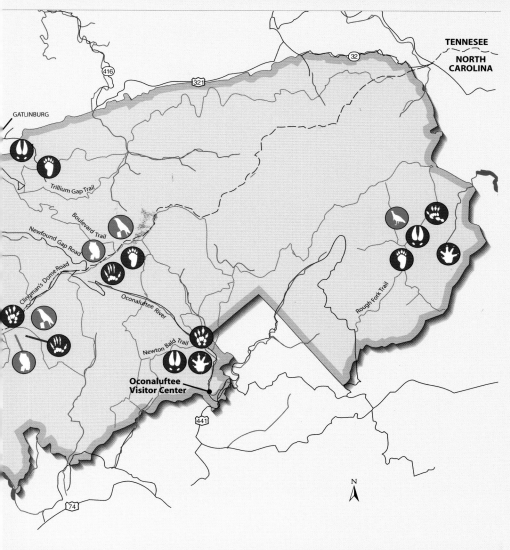

TENNESSEE
NORTH CAROLINA

GATLINBURG

Trillium Gap Trail

Boulevard Trail

Newfound Gap Road

Clingman's Dome Road

Oconaluftee River

Newton Bald Trail

Rough Fork Trail

Oconaluftee Visitor Center

N

 River Otter

 White-tailed Deer

 Wild Boar

 Wild Turkey

——River

——Trail

——Road
Some roads impassable
in winter or when wet

INTRODUCTION

Humbling in its magnitude and breathtaking in its beauty, the Great Smoky Mountains National Park is an old and timeless land. A primeval blue mist hangs in the valleys. The jagged peaks of Chimney Tops tell of the distant past and millions of years of intense pressures that buckled and tilted the earth's crust to form steep cliffs and solitary pinnacles. The massive hemlocks along LeConte Creek are ancient sentries that tower more than a hundred feet tall and have been witness to the change from the land of the Cherokee to a land of settlers and farmers and, finally, to one of this country's most popular national parks.

There is a magnetic aura to the Great Smoky Mountains. In fact, each year over 8 million visitors flock to this sanctuary of over 500,000 acres that has become America's most visited national park. Many visitors seek solitude and the rejuvenation of spirit that only nature can provide. The park's forests are home to approximately 1,500 species of flowering plants and over 100 species of trees. The wildlife of the park is just as plentiful with over 200 species of birds, 70 species of mammals, and over 50 species of reptiles and amphibians.

In the dense forests of the Smokies, wildlife species usually offer just a glimpse of themselves. The red squirrel provides a brief view as it sprints from tree to tree. Salamanders are almost always hidden and only seen by those who discover their nesting pools. It is in open spaces, such as Cade's Cove, that wildlife reveal themselves for closer scrutiny. Visitors will discover that the park relinquishes its wildlife secrets only to those who are patient and observant.

The forests of the Smokies require visitors to be in tune with their surroundings in order to see the wildlife residents. The forests have many stories to tell. A small trail running through tall grass may lead visitors to the home of a deer mouse. Disturbed leaves on the forest floor may tell of a feeding flock of wild turkeys that has recently passed by. Animal signs tell us stories that can lead us to the animals themselves.

Visitors will also see more wildlife if they understand what animals are found in a particular area and what features attract them to that area. The abundant grasses and shrubs of Cade's Cove attract feeding white-tailed deer and in turn the deer attract predators such as the coyote and red wolf. The species accounts in this book should give you an idea of what animals to look for and their locations.

This wildlife watcher's guide is an invitation for park visitors to be more than "sleepwalkers," as Henry David Thoreau called us; we should awaken to the wild creatures around us—watch with fascination the nest-building skills of the ruby-throated hummingbird, listen intently to the song of the goldfinch—and take pleasure in the simple acts of nature.

TIPS FOR WILDLIFE WATCHERS

In the park's dense woodlands an animal is seldom completely visible. So look for parts of the wildlife: the flick of a white-tailed deer's ear or the twitch of a bobcat's tail. And don't forget to use *all* of your senses. You might hear some animals before you see them. You may smell a black bear or skunk approaching from downwind before its arrival.

You can also search for the evidence of animals, such as tracks, scats, or nests. Patiently waiting near a bird's nest will many times afford a glimpse as the bird returns to its daily routine. Small animals, although less conspicuous, are very rewarding to see. The deer mouse, like the white-tailed deer, follows established trails. After a summer shower, watch for the paths of the eft stage of the newt.

Subtle yet visible color differences also abound in nature. The dark color of the black bear may provide excellent camouflage in the shade of a rhododendron but may sharply contrast against the green pastures of Cade's Cove.

But remember that not all wildlife present themselves at eye level so look up, down, and all around. You can see both the soaring hawk and the scurrying chipmunk by observing nature with a broader perspective.

Also, use your car for a blind. Most wildlife in the park are accustomed to seeing vehicles pass through the park and do not feel threatened. Stay in your car to witness the daily routine of animals, which may seem oblivious to your presence. Your car is also a safe haven from a protective bear with cubs.

You can find some of the Smokies' best-viewing opportunities in the park's more remote areas, such as Cataloochee. Take the time to leave your car and look for some of the park's less-often-seen wildlife, such as small mammals and songbirds. And don't forget your binoculars for viewing distant wildlife.

It's important to match wildlife to its habitat. Know what animals to expect to see. For example, when you go to Cade's Cove in June, expect to see white-tailed deer, groundhogs, Eastern bluebirds, wild turkeys, or the rare red wolf. At Clingman's Dome, expect to see common ravens and red squirrels.

Be as silent as possible while attempting to view wildlife. Animals are in tune with their surroundings and noisy intruders are rarely rewarded with wildlife sightings. You will also need to exercise patience because wildlife in the park does not always appear on cue.

A WILDLIFE WATCHER'S CODE OF CONDUCT

In 1916 the National Park Service adopted the following mandate to guide the management of the Great Smoky Mountains National Park:

> . . . to conserve the scenery and the natural and historic objects and the wildlife therein, and to provide for the enjoyment of the same in such a manner and by such means as will leave them unimpaired for the enjoyment of future generations.

If we are to leave the many species of wildlife found in the Great Smoky Mountains in a "unimpaired" state, the more than 8 million visitors per year must play a large role by following park rules and reacting responsibly when encountering and viewing wildlife.

Don't feed the wildlife

Feeding black bears or any other wildlife species is illegal in the park because it can prove dangerous for both visitor and animal. Feeding wildlife does not tame the animal but instead reinforces behavior that can be harmful to them. Wild animals that have become habituated to being fed by humans learn to depend on that food source and will, in the case of a black bear, take food even when it isn't offered, thus leading to an encounter that can be injurious to the park visitor. A raccoon was recently seen in Cade's Cove dangerously approaching every passing car for a handout. It was a reminder of how we can reduce the "wildness" of animals and possibly endanger their lives when the lean winter months drive away a primary food source—the park visitor.

Watch from a safe distance

Many of the animals in the park are somewhat tolerant of park visitors; for that reason wildlife viewing in the Smokies can be rewarding. Vehicles make a great nonthreatening blind that many animals simply ignore. Watching from a safe distance is also a courtesy to other visitors because once an animal's comfort zone is compromised by an intruding visitor, it will seek sanctuary at a less congested site. It is also against park regulations to harass or approach wildlife.

Photographing wildlife

A camera lens is not a permit to bend park rules. Carry the correct photographic equipment to avoid approaching wildlife too closely. Remember that no "once-in-a-lifetime shot" justifies injuring wildlife or other park visitors.

Drive defensively

Posted speed limits are actively enforced within the Smokies because many animals cross the roadways within the park. Deer do not look both ways before crossing the street. Driving the posted limits also improves wildlife viewing opportunities. Narrow one-lane roads, such as those in Abrams Creek or Cade's Cove, are not designed to accommodate faster-moving cars. Be sure to utilize the many pull-offs found on park roads to observe or photograph wildlife. The Great Smoky Mountains provide an opportunity to slow down and enjoy the scenery and wildlife. Expect slow-moving traffic, particularly on busy spring and fall weekends when it may take several hours to travel the Cade's Cove loop road.

Bear-proof your camp

Because the Great Smoky Mountains contain one of the highest densities of black bears in the eastern United States, bear-proofing your camp is essential. Backpackers are required to hang their food at least 10 feet off the ground and 4 feet from the nearest tree, or to use bear-resistant containers. Rent or purchase the containers at Sugarlands and Oconaluftee visitor centers. Campers using developed campgrounds should follow a few simple guidelines: Keep the camp clean, use the bear-resistant trash cans provided throughout the park, and store food in a vehicle trunk. These simple precautions will prevent unwanted foraging in your camp by bears, raccoons, or skunks.

Pets

Although pets are permitted in some areas of the park, they must be under the constant physical control of their owner. They are prohibited on all park trails. Noisy pets make viewing of wildlife difficult.

Do not harass wildlife

The use of artificial calls and spotlights, often used by poachers, is strictly prohibited. Poaching is a serious threat to the park's wildlife populations. A recent broken poaching ring netted the confiscation of over 250 gallbladders of black bears that were poached to support an overseas "traditional" medicine industry. In 1991 two men were arrested for poaching two large bucks in Cade's Cove. The deer, nicknamed "Streamer" and "Tim's Ten," were two of the park's most photographed deer. Park rangers welcome information on people using spotlights or calls so that the rangers can better protect the Smokies' wildlife.

Fishing

With more than a thousand miles of clear streams, fishing is a major recreational activity in the park. A reciprocal agreement exists allowing the acceptance of North Carolina and Tennessee fishing licenses on any open park stream. Only single-hook artificial flies or lures are allowed. The use of live bait or preserved baits, such as salmon eggs or corn, is prohibited. Many of the higher-elevation streams are closed to fishing in order to protect the native brook trout population. The possession of a brook trout is prohibited in the park. A detailed fishing regulation pamphlet is available from the park headquarters.

You can also take advantage of the many educational programs and exhibits offered in the Smokies. A park ranger or local expert is a good source for wildlife information.

Hiking

The mountains and forests of the Great Smoky Mountains National Park invite visitors to explore and seek out the hidden gems of nature. To make any trip safer and more enjoyable, be sure to stay on the trails, and use the "buddy system"—don't hike alone. Never go hiking in the dark.

In the often rugged terrain, it is important to be careful. Always drink plenty of purified water and eat high-energy foods, especially on extended hikes.

Because the temperatures can change suddenly and dramatically, be sure to dress appropriately. Clothing layers can be added or taken off as the weather warrants—be prepared for rain and snow.

Also, know your limitations. Choose trails that match your skills, and give yourself plenty of time to make your destination.

HABITATS

One of the best ways to find wildlife in the Smokies is to understand that each forest type attracts a specific group of wildlife species. In turn, elevation and moisture affect the distribution of forest types. About sixteen peaks in the park have elevations over 6,000 feet. Visitors can pass through forests that are typical of latitudes from New England through the Southeast in the short drive between Sugarlands and Clingman's Dome. Old growth and virgin timber can be found on about 20 percent of the park. The following forest types harbor the wildlife that call the Great Smoky Mountains home.

Spruce-fir—Dominated by red spruce and Fraser fir, this forest type is found in the park's highest sections. Although it can extend to lower altitudes, this forest is generally found above the 4,500-foot elevation. Wildlife attracted to these areas are often unique to the spruce-fir forest, typically being found more often to the north of the park. This forest attracts the red squirrel, common raven and bobcat.

Northern Hardwood—This deciduous forest type, which is a high-elevation forest found above 4,500 feet, is characterized by beech trees and yellow birch. This forest also attracts northern species of wildlife such as the black-capped chickadee and gray squirrel.

Cove Hardwood—Huge old growth stands and pure stands of yellow poplar trees are common within this forest type. This forest is found below 4,500 feet in the park's sheltered valleys. Basswood and mountain silverbell are also common trees in this forest. These rich valleys attract one of the park's most well-known wildlife species, the black bear, and other wildlife such as barred owls and pileated woodpeckers.

Hemlock—This forest occurs below 4,000 feet and around moist areas in the park, especially along sheltered streams. Tall, often huge, Canadian hemlocks are the most common tree species. Rhododendron and flame azalea are common understory shrubs. These streamside locations attract ruby-throated hummingbirds and belted kingfishers, birds typical of dense evergreen forests and large numbers of amphibians dependent on the forest's waters, such as the red-spotted newt.

Grassy and Heath Balds—Found in the highest sections of the park, balds are grassy or shrubby areas that support very little tall plant growth. Shrubby plant growth includes well-known displays of flame azaleas on Gregory Bald and Catawba rhododendrons on Andrews Bald. Having high elevations, these open areas attract many species of wildlife and are good locations to watch for soaring birds such as common ravens, turkey vultures, and migrating hawks.

Oak and Pine—At lower and middle elevations, dry, shallow soil supports oak and pine forests that have distinctive understory plants such as flame azaleas and mountain laurel. Maple, locust, pine, and hickory trees also abound. This forest type can be scattered throughout the park in areas below the 5,000-foot elevation. These forests attract wildlife species such as white-tailed deer and wild turkey, that are dependent on the large volume of nuts.

It is important to note that while each of these forest types are mentioned in this guidebook, there are no clear boundary lines in nature. The forests of the Smokies are in constant transition with the spruce-fir forest blending into the northern hardwood forest which blends into the cove hardwood forest.

INTERESTING NOTES

Several species of wildlife that once roamed the Smoky Mountains have become extinct since the first European immigrants settled in the area. The fisher, bison, and gray wolf once roamed the park and are now extinct. The mountain lion has been considered extinct in the park since the 1920s. Reports of lion sightings, however, still occur. The existence of a small remnant population of escaped or released lions is possible. But unless concrete evidence is presented, the status of the mountain lion is unlikely to change.

The red wolf, peregrine falcon, and river otter have been re-introduced into the park in an effort to re-establish wildlife populations that were present before settlement of the area. The elk is presently being evaluated for reintroduction. The wild boar is an exotic animal from Europe that was accidentally introduced into the park.

The rainbow trout was introduced into park streams in the late 1950s. This introduction caused the extinction of the smoky madtom, a small catfish. A small remnant population of the smoky madtom was discovered in 1980. Descendants from this population were released into Abrams Creek in the late 1980s in hope of re-establishing a viable population in their former homes.

The brown trout, once stocked in the park, has migrated into many park streams. The native brook trout has also suffered from loss of habitat caused by early logging operations and by failing to compete with the larger non-native trout that have been released. The park service is currently trying to establish pure brook trout streams.

WILDLIFE WATCHING HOT SPOTS

Much of the park is accessible by trail; few roads, however, penetrate this eastern wilderness. The following destinations provide the best wildlife-viewing opportunities on the Tennessee and North Carolina sides of the park for the visitor that cannot make the lengthy hikes required to access remote sections of the park.

Tennessee

Abrams Creek—Located on the western border, this hidden valley has the park's lowest altitude at 857 feet. Large hemlock trees line the creek, which was the site of river otter re-introductions in the late 1980s. You can easily observe the aquatic life in the stream. In early May, look for the spawning activity of darters and hog suckers. Muskrats and skunks may frequent the streamside. Watch for wild boar and coyote on the hiking trail to Cade's Cove. You can find American goldfinch and migrating warblers near the parking area. The surrounding oak and pine forest exhibits an abundance of wildflowers such as mountain laurel, dwarf crested iris, and fire pink.

Cade's Cove—This secluded valley is widely know as one of the park's most scenic venues. It is also the best location for viewing many species of wildlife. You can also see white-tailed deer, groundhogs, and wild turkeys in the central pastures of the Cove. Occasionally, you can see coyotes and the recently introduced red wolf. Black bears may appear at the edge of the oak and pine forests that line the Cove's outer fringes. Limestone sinks provide seasonal pools of water for many species of amphibians that call the Cove home. The pastures, which still support grazing herds of cattle, are home to many species of open country birds such as the Eastern bluebird. The 11-mile loop road provides easy access to areas frequented by wildlife in the Cove. The Cove's southern portion, which is the farthest from the campground, is often the best area for wildlife observation. Hyatt Lane is a two-lane dirt road that runs through the heart of the Cove's pastures and is a good location for observing wildlife. Avoid heavy crowds and discover more wildlife by visiting the Cove early and late in the day.

Sugarlands—The Sugarlands area is home to the main, northern entrance to the park. The park headquarters and the Sugarlands visitor center are located within this area. The visitor center houses a gift shop and educational exhibits on the park's natural wonders. This area is also an ideal place to observe wildlife. The sheltered valley at the 1,500-foot elevation consists of a forest with scattered pines and hardwood trees. Hemlock stands shade the west prong of the Little Pigeon River and Fighting Creek. The quiet walk between the visitor center and the park headquarters is located in a shady hemlock grove that is home to a

number of white-tailed deer. The trail is lined with a shower of ephemeral spring wildflowers such as Virginia bluebells. Birding in this area can lead to the sighting of numerous species. Both red and gray squirrels have been found in this area.

Foothills Parkway—Managed by the National Park Service, the Foothills Parkway runs along the top of Chilhowee Mountain, which parallels the park's northwestern boundary near Townsend. Look Rock, located near Townsend, provides vistas of the western slope of the Smokies and the adjacent foothills. The area is well-known for migrating birds of prey. In one day during the fall, as many as one thousand raptors have been seen migrating overhead. From the observation tower, red-tailed hawks and turkey vultures can often be seen riding the thermal updrafts.

Roaring Fork Motor Trail—The route of the motor trail traverses steep valleys that were once home to the Roaring Fork community where mountain farmers scraped out an existence in the shallow rocky soil. Tall groves of gray-trunked, yellow poplar now stand where a farm once stood. With an elevation of around 2,100 feet, the area is covered by cove hardwood forests, oak and pine forests, and hemlock stands. Tall hemlock trees shelter the Roaring Fork and LeConte Creek where the remains of massive American chestnut trees, victims of an exotic blight, litter the ground. Some of these fallen giants may have been 5 or 6 feet in diameter. One can only imagine what this forest was like with such giant sentries. The trail to Mount LeConte and Rainbow Falls is strenuous but worth the effort. The area is well-known for its dazzling display of spring wildflowers such as the large-flowered trillium. Look for white-tailed deer and an occasional black bear in the lower elevations where you will also find yellow poplar groves. You will see Eastern chipmunks and gray squirrels scurrying over rocks and fallen trees. The single-lane road does not lend itself to a quick pace; you may need an hour to travel the 5.5 miles. To best observe this area's wildlife, use the numerous pull-offs along the Motor Trail.

North Carolina

Appalachian Trail—Running along the top of the Smokies, the Appalachian Trail is a north-south trail that runs from northern Georgia into Maine. The trail embraces the highest ridgelines along the North Carolina and Tennessee border. Highlights of the trail include the spruce-fir forest, grassy balds, and uninterrupted scenic vistas. Because of its length and location, it is not an easy trail, but it is a popular destination that attracts many overnight backpackers. The wildlife to watch for include red squirrel, black bear, and common raven.

Newfound Gap and **Clingman's Dome**—These high-elevation locations are found at the apex of the Newfound Gap Road that connects Gatlinburg, Tennessee, and Cherokee, North Carolina.

Newfound Gap is located at an elevation of 5,040 feet and is surrounded by northern hardwood forest and thick stands of spruce-fir forest. The flora and fauna here are, in many cases, at the southern limit of their range and are normally found farther north of the park in eastern Canada. Watch for bird life typical of high-altitude locations, such as the common raven and black-capped chickadee. The Appalachian Trail crosses at the parking lot and is a good place to see red squirrels. The weather here is always substantially cooler than in surrounding areas and the wind constantly blows through the Gap. The Newfound Gap Road is often closed during winter months when high-altitude snowstorms make the road impassable.

The highest point in the park is Clingman's Dome with an elevation of 6,643 feet. The road accessing Clingman's Dome is located a short distance east of the Newfound Gap parking area and south of the Newfound Gap Road. Red spruce and Fraser fir dominate the spruce-fir forest; pure stands of Fraser fir being found at the highest elevations. More than 90 percent of the firs from these pure stands are now dead. The woolly balsam adelgid, an exotic aphid-like insect, has devastated the park's fir trees. Their dead silver trunks stand as mute testimony of how, like the American chestnut, the smallest of exotic pests can destroy whole tree populations. Many species of wildlife are found only in this high forest. The impact on species dependent on the spruce-fir forest remains to be seen. Look for groundhogs and red squirrels along the road to the top.

Cataloochee—The historic community of Cataloochee is off the beaten path but is a very worthwhile destination. A dirt road just off Interstate 40 at exit 20 leads to Cataloochee Valley; it is only 11 miles long but takes almost an hour to drive. The road is narrow and winding but does not require a four-wheel-drive vehicle. A second entrance road, which enters the valley from Big Creek, is 5 miles longer and just as winding. The Cataloochee Valley is much like Cade's Cove. It has several historic buildings scattered around the Valley. The main difference between the two sites is the number of visitors; not as many people go to Cataloochee. The Valley is also narrower and lacks the wide pastures of Cade's Cove. At 2,600 feet in elevation, it is also higher. The cove hardwood forest of the area is known for its huge poplar trees and extravagant wildflower displays. This area provides spectacular scenery and relative solitude, and you may see black bears and deer feeding in abandoned orchards.

Oconaluftee Valley—Located just north of Cherokee, North Carolina, the Valley is a scenic, educational area with a pastoral setting on the banks of the Oconaluftee River. The Pioneer Farmstead has buildings that were built in the late 1700s. The many pastures provide homes for open-country bird species such as the red-winged blackbird, wild turkey and barn swallows, as well as open-country mammals such as the white-tailed deer, groundhog, red fox, and, occasionally, black bear. Hardwood and pine forests surround these low-elevation meadows that average 2,000 feet above sea level.

WILDLIFE ENCOUNTERS

The following chart will help you estimate the liklihood of seeing various species on your visit to Great Smoky Mountains National Park.

■ **Common**   On any given day, you should see this species.

◪ **Irregular**   The species is not as common, and you must try a little harder to find it.

☐ **Rare**   It's still possible to find the species if you use the suggestions given in this book and have a little luck.

MAMMALS

Black Bear	◪	Gray Squirrel	■	Red Wolf	☐
Bobcat	☐	Groundhog	■	River Otter	☐
Coyote	◪	Opossum	■	Striped Skunk	■
Deer Mouse	■	Raccoon	■	White-tailed Deer	■
Eastern Chipmunk	■	Red Fox	◪	Wild Boar	■
Eastern Cottontail Rabbit	■	Red Squirrel	■		

BIRDS

American Goldfinch	■	Downy Woodpecker	◪	Red-winged Blackbird	◪
Barn Swallow	■	Eastern Bluebird	■	Rose-breasted Grosbeak	■
Barred Owl	◪	Eastern Screech Owl	◪	Ruby-throated Hummingbird	■
Belted Kingfisher	◪	Pileated Woodpecker	◪	Tufted Titmouse	■
Carolina Chickadee	■	Red-bellied Woodpecker	■	Turkey Vulture	◪
Common Raven	■	Red-tailed Hawk	◪	Wild Turkey	◪

REPTILES

Northern Copperhead	◪	Northern Fence Lizard	■	Timber Rattlesnake	◪

AMPHIBIANS

American Toad	◪	Longtail Salamander	◪	Wood Frog	◪
Gray Treefrog	◪	Red-spotted Newt	◪	Spotted Salamander	◪
Jordan's Salamander	◪	Southern Appalachian Slimy Salamander	◪		

Always remember there are no guarantees in wildlife watching—but that is what makes each sighting an adventure!

Successful wildlife encounters require knowledge of the animal's habits and habitats, when and where to look for them, and a great deal of patience. Remember: Avoid any behavior on your part that would bring stress to wildlife, and don't get too close.

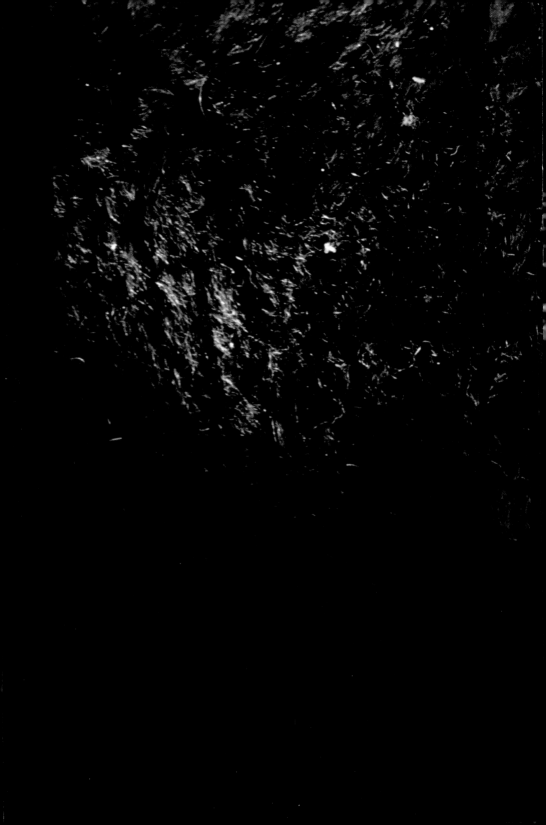

MAMMALS

BLACK BEAR

No single wildlife species symbolizes the Great Smoky Mountains more than the black bear (*Ursus americanus*). It is the largest remaining animal found within the park. Averaging between 120 and 250 pounds, it is the smallest of North America's bears. An estimated 400 to 600 bears within the park's boundaries represent one of the highest densities of black bears found in North America. Black bears are outstanding climbers and often avoid danger by scaling trees. Although the color phases of the black bear vary from black to brown to silver, black bears in the East are almost completely black.

Bears are opportunistic omnivores, but they prefer vegetation and fruits. The black bear possesses relatively poor eyesight but has an acute sense of smell, which aids in finding food. Normally active at night but can be seen at anytime. It is considered a strong swimmer with excellent fishing skills. On land, the black bear is capable of running at speeds up to 30 mph. The over 500,000 acres of the Great Smoky Mountains are important for an animal that can wander 20 miles in a day. The mature forest offers many den trees and heavy nut-producing trees, such as oaks, which are essential to a healthy bear population. Through consuming large amounts of this tree's fruits, bears add fat reserves.

During the winter season, bears go into a semi-hibernation state. Although they are capable of waking, they prefer to sleep. Dens can be found in rocky overhangs and deadfalls (hollow fallen trees). Due to the old-growth nature of much of the forests in the Smokies, however, dens are often located high in hollows of mature hardwood trees.

So it follows that during the winter, bear sightings are unusual—unless warm weather prompts a bear to take a walk. The females have already given birth to one to three cubs. The young cubs, weighing 7 to 12 ounces, are born helpless. They emerge for the first time from the den in the spring. By this time, they weigh about 4 pounds and have opened their eyes.

Throughout the country, the poaching of black bears for their gallbladders and other body parts has caused a decline in bear populations. Each year poachers illegally take about 50 to 80 bears from the park. However, biologists felt the population was strong enough within the park to relocate a few bears to the Big South Fork National Park as part of a reintroduction project that began in 1996.

You can look for several signs of black bears. The bear's tracks are 5 inches across, showing five digits and a large foot pad. Foraging bears rip open rotting logs in search of insect larvae.

Black bears often leave their claw marks on boundary trees as a sign of territoriality.

Note that there are several good reasons to avoid approaching a bear too closely—even for that once-in-a-lifetime photograph. To compromise the wildness of a bear by making it accustomed to human contact could spell doom for the individual bear. Bad habits in bears, such as an association of humans with food, are hard to break and could eventually cost a bear its life. Sow bears are particularly temperamental when they have cubs around. Possessing short, sharp claws and extraordinary strength, the black bear is a formidable foe when it feels threatened or cornered.

Where To Find Black Bears

Sightings of black bears are sporadic and unpredictable. But they have been seen along the Newfound Gap Road between Sugarlands and Oconaluftee, Clingman's Dome Road, Cosby Campground, Roaring Fork Motor Trail, and around the Cade's Cove Loop Road.

Roadsides in the park are common areas for bear sightings. Bears tend to prefer the more remote reaches of the park, however, making backcountry trails good places to look for them. Bears also occasionally frequent campgrounds and trail shelters.

EASTERN COTTONTAIL RABBIT

The Eastern cottontail rabbit (*Sylvilagus floridanus*) gets its name from its distinctive white tail, which it flashes when threatened. It is commonly found in all elevations of the park. The cottontail rabbit possesses powerful hind legs and large ears that are up to 3 inches in length. It has a rusty nape and sports mixed shades of light and dark-brown that give the cottontail a brownish-gray color overall. The cottontail weighs between 2 and 4 pounds and is about 1 foot long.

The cottontail is a favorite meal of most predators in the Smokies, from timber rattlesnakes to great-horned owls, so it must be constantly alert for predators from the air and land. Large eyes set on the sides of the animal's head provide a wide view of its surroundings from behind and in front. During the daylight hours, rabbits rest motionless in hidden depressions, or forms, and depend on their color to hide them. When they are flushed from these forms, the cottontail follows a zigzag course to the next patch of cover.

Because cottontails are a major prey species, they need to be prolific. Between late February and September, cottontail rabbits produce four to seven young per litter and up to four litters per year. The young are born blind, naked, and defenseless in a fur-lined nest. They each have a distinct white spot between their ears that they lose as adults. The loss of each year's young due to predation and other mortality factors exceeds 80 percent. As a result, few rabbits live more than a year. A high mortality rate is necessary with such a reproductive animal; otherwise, a single pair of rabbits could cause the population to reach about 350,000 cottontails in just five years.

Where To Find Eastern Cottontail Rabbits

Cottontails are active early and late in the day. They are most often seen feeding in grassy areas alongside park roads and in fields and pastures during early evening and at night.

RED WOLF

One of North America's most endangered species is now pioneering lands in the Great Smoky Mountains that have not seen a wolf in nearly one hundred years. The red wolf (*Canis rufus*), which was once extinct from the Smoky Mountains, plays an important role in the strategy of nature. Captive-reared populations have been returned to the wild in coastal North Carolina and the Great Smoky Mountains.

Red wolves resemble the coyote, another relatively new resident of the park. In many cases, only an expert can tell the difference between a juvenile red wolf (one less than two years old) and an adult coyote. Coyotes generally do not exceed 40 pounds in weight; red wolf females weigh between 45 and 55 pounds and males between 55 and 65 pounds. Red wolves also have a more robust body shape. Some field guides indicate that coyotes run with their tail between their legs as opposed to the wolf which holds its tail high, but this trait is not always reliable. Adult wolves are darker red than the coyote.

Red wolves seem to lack the social development of the gray wolf, which has well organized social structures in the Park including dominant males and females. While red wolves may seem to have a dominant male and female, they are usually just parents, and are not disposed to establishing dominance over subordinate wolves. Packs of red wolves appear to be family units that do not tolerate outside wolves. Red wolves, which are shy and retiring, often wander in solitude. Young male pups leave the pack after one year, but young females often stay with the parents to help rear the next litter.

Red wolves feed primarily on small mammals; they are opportunistic predators, however, and have been known to kill black bear cubs. There are also indications that they kill wild boars. They are unbelievably quick, which makes them such efficient predators.

Wolves are known to be wanderers; and red wolves are no exception. They are wide-ranging and can cover many miles in a day.

This habit may change in the park as their population rises and more wolves establish territories.

The U.S. Fish and Wildlife Service has released red wolves in the park at Cade's Cove, Elkmont, and Tremont. This reintroduction has met with success and failure. In the past, deaths have resulted from the transmission of parvo-virus to wild-born pups that were not vaccinated.

Rangers hope the park and surrounding national forests will hold between 25 and 50 mated pairs of wolves. If a viable population is to flourish, it will have to develop some immunity to the stresses and diseases that are present in the wild.

Where To Find Red Wolves

Red wolves may be found in Cade's Cove near Hyatt Lane. Some may be wearing colored radio collars. Although they are wide-ranging animals, it is not common to see a red wolf.

The Smokies are a more complete ecosystem for the red wolf, and the possibility of seeing a wolf in the wild increases the mystique and appeal of the park.

RACCOON

It is hard to confuse the raccoon (*Procyon lotor*) with any other animal in the park. The black facial markings, which resemble a mask, and the bushy black-and-tan-ringed tail are characteristic of the raccoon. Its body is tan with a salt-and-pepper color. Large male raccoons can weigh up to 35 pounds. Because they are distant relatives to the bear family, raccoon males are referred to as boars, and females as sows. A raccoon's front feet or "hands" are almost human-like and are extremely dexterous. The front feet leave tracks that resemble a person's handprint, while the hind foot leaves broad, flat tracks like that of the bear.

The tracks can be found along most streams in the park. Raccoons are often seen hunched over and waddling at night as they scurry through campgrounds. They have an inquisitive nature that makes them a very popular species of wildlife. Although they seem to be begging, it is important to keep your distance because they are one of the few animals in the park that can carry both canine distemper and rabies.

The name "raccoon" is derived from the Algonquian name arakunem, which means "hand scratcher," and the specific Latin name *lotor*, which means "washer." Both of these names are in reference to the raccoon's peculiar dining habit: It appears to wash its food before eating. This action may actually be an innate foraging pattern rather than washing.

The nocturnal raccoon is most commonly seen foraging for food at night. It is omnivorous, and eats berries, nuts, persimmons, frogs, birds, salamanders, and snakes.

The raccoon's den is primarily in a hollow log or tree. The offspring are born in April and May in litters of about four babies. The female's twittering chatter can often be heard as she prods the young to safety. When threatened, the raccoon will snarl and growl like a dog.

Where To Find Raccoons

Raccoons can be found at all elevations. But since much of their foraging occurs near the water, they are more common at lower elevations. Raccoons may be found at Oconaluftee, Greenbrier, Sugarlands, Elkmont, and Cade's Cove.

GROUNDHOG

The groundhog (*Marmota monax*) is also referred to as a woodchuck. It dines on the succulent grasses at the edges of park roads and pastures, such as those in Cade's Cove. The groundhog is up to 2 feet in length and weighs up to 10 pounds. It is a short-legged and heavy-bodied animal that seems to ripple when it dashes for cover. Like its cousin the prairie dog, the groundhog whistles or barks an alarm when danger is near. Its fur is a salt-and-pepper color with an orange-tinted belly.

These strong diggers develop extensive underground burrows. From October to February, the groundhog hibernates there. Dens usually have two or more entrances and can extend more than 5 feet into the ground. Each year, two to six young are born in these underground sanctuaries. Groundhogs climb trees to dine on the buds and bark. While on the ground it dines on grasses and succulent plants.

Where To Find Groundhogs

The groundhog has been found at most locations in the park. Most frequently, they can be found near old agricultural fields and pastures, such as those in Cade's Cove and Oconaluftee.

RED FOX

The red fox (*Vulpes vulpes*) is the more unusual of the park's two species of fox and can be easily distinguished from the gray fox (*Urocyon cinereoargenteus*). The red fox has a white tip on its tail, and its feet and legs are almost black. The gray fox, on the other hand, has a black-tipped tail and a gray body with some black-and-white fur; it also has a black stripe down its back. The red fox, which has acutely pointed ears and nose, is the size of a small dog and is usually a rusty-red color. Colors vary, however, from light tan to black. Adult animals weigh between 10 and 15 pounds.

The reputation of the fox for being clever is well founded. They are quite resourceful, learn quickly, and are extremely cautious. They may have three or more entrances to their dens to provide a quick exodus from intruders such as coyotes. Foxes have difficulty competing with coyotes, which chase and harass them.

Red foxes are born during March and April in underground dens; four to nine young are born in each litter. Males remain attentive to the female and bring food for the young after their birth.

It is debated whether the red fox is native to the park or an introduced exotic species. Hunters introduced the red fox into nearby areas, and these animals could have immigrated to the park. Red fox do not appear to have been present in the park prior to white settlement of the area, but they could have emigrated from the north of the park where they were known to exist. The red fox has now filled a niche in the park as a consumer of mice, small mammals, and fruits.

Where To Find Red Foxes

Not seeming to show a real preference for any particular area in the park, the red fox can be found at all elevations. They are an uncommon sighting because of their shy, secretive nature. Yet they are occasionally seen crossing park roads at night.

COYOTE

In many Native American legends, the coyote (*Canis latrans*) is known as the trickster. It is an animal that is both revered and maligned throughout the western parts of the United States. This wild canid is a relative newcomer to the Great Smoky Mountains. Coyotes were first reported in the area in 1947 at Cherokee, North Carolina. They began to colonize the park in the early 1980s and are most common in the western third of the park. Coyote colonization was made possible by the extinction of several large predators, such as gray wolves and the Eastern cougar, native to the park. This allowed the coyote to effectively fill the role of top predator.

The coyote, which looks like a small shepherd dog, weighs between 20 and 40 pounds. It has a grizzled light tan coat, pointed nose, and bushy tail that lacks the curl a domestic shepherd possesses. The coyote stands about 30 inches tall at the shoulder.

There are no genetic differences between coyotes found in the East and those in the West. The coyotes found in the park differ from their western cousins in small behavioral and physical ways. Eastern coyotes are less "talkative" and are only occasionally heard vocalizing in the manner that has earned the Western coyote the nickname "song dog." Eastern coyotes can sometimes be heard uttering excited yips when reuniting with other family members.

Coyotes usually hunt alone. They are extremely fast, and capable of running at speeds of up to 40 mph. Although primarily nocturnal hunters, they will hunt during the day. Coyotes in the park feed predominantly on small mammals, such as deer mice and rabbits. They will also feast on an occasional white-tailed deer fawn or insects such as grasshoppers.

In early spring, coyote pups are born in litters of five to ten in underground dens found in banks and, occasionally, old groundhog holes. The den is a wide-mouthed hole that extends up to 20 feet and ends in a nesting chamber. Adult coyotes usually mate for several years or maintain a lifelong bond.

Where To Find Coyotes

Coyotes are most often found in the southern sections of the park around and in the pastures of Cade's Cove. They have also been found around Abrams Creek. They are seen in the early morning and late afternoon foraging around the forest and field edges, and they can be seen crossing park roads at night.

BOBCAT

The name "bobcat" refers to this animal's short 5-inch tail, which has a black tip. Although it is extremely secretive and rarely seen, the bobcat (*Felis rufus*) is a fairly common resident of the Great Smoky Mountains. It is the park's only verifiably present species of cat. Adult bobcats average 20 pounds, but large males may weigh up to 35 pounds. The bobcats' colors blend so well with their surroundings that it is virtually impossible to see them unless they are moving. They are generally a mottled dark and light tan; some bobcats, however, are a much darker gray.

The bobcat's eyes glow a bright yellow color at night and are adapted for its nocturnal hunting habits; the irises expand widely to let in available light.

A silent stealthy hunter, the bobcat dines regularly on cottontail rabbits, birds, and even deer fawns. Bobcats sometimes cover their kill with leaves and debris. This is especially true if the prey is a large animal, such as a deer, which the bobcat cannot completely consume in one feeding. Bobcats are excellent climbers but do most of their hunting on the ground.

During the late winter mating season, bobcats have been known to vocalize loudly. Its squall is eerie and sounds like a high-pitched scream.

In the spring, two to three young bobcats are born in dens under rock outcroppings or in hollow logs. The young leave their mother for a solitary life in the autumn after their birth.

Where To Find Bobcats

It is impossible to predict where a bobcat might be seen. Sightings have been documented at locations from Cade's Cove to Clingman's Dome. Young bobcats, which have not yet developed the stealth of adults, can sometimes be seen in late summer and early fall after they have struck out on their own.

OPOSSUM

The opossum (*Didelphis marsupialis*), which is the size of a house cat, is the park's only marsupial, or pouched animal. It has a tail that measures up to 20 inches and a pointed, pink nose. A large male weighs up to 14 pounds.

The name "opossum" originated from the Algonquian word apasum, which means "the white animal" and refers to its white face, fur, and belly. While the opossum's range has extended northward, extremely cold climates pose the threat of frostbite on its paper-thin ears, naked tail, and exposed nose. The tail is used to store fat reserves to survive the lean winter.

The opossum has several physical characteristics that make it well adapted to its tree-bound lifestyle. The hind foot has a nail-less, opposable thumb that allows it to grasp tree limbs and food. The tail is used to hang from trees.

Because the opossum is a marsupial, it raises its young in a pouch on its belly. The young are born in litters of up to fourteen opossums, and each measures only 1/4 of an inch at birth—about the size of a garden pea. After two months, the young opossums emerge from the pouch and climb onto their mother's back and cling to her hair when traveling.

The opossum has an extraordinarily large number of teeth compared to other mammals. It may hiss and show all fifty teeth if it feels threatened; this makes the animal appear to be grinning, which has led to the phrase "grinning like a possum." The phrase "playing possum" comes from the animal's defensive habit of feigning death when it is threatened or harassed.

The opossum is a nocturnal animal and an extremely opportunistic feeder that dines on a number of plants and animals. Because they even eat roadside carrion, a large number of animals are killed by cars.

Where To Find Opossums

Opossums may be found at Cade's Cove, Oconaluftee, and Cataloochee at all elevations in the park, although it is more common at lower elevations.

RIVER OTTER

The classic image of the river otter (*Lutra canadensis*) is that of a playful creature frolicking on river banks or sliding on its belly. Although these entertaining antics serve a function, the animal does seem to be enjoying itself. The otter is a full-time resident of streams and rivers of the Great Smoky Mountains.

River otters are native to the streams of the park. By the time the park was established in the mid-1930s, however, the otter was gone. On the Tennessee side of the park, they are listed as a threatened species. Habitat loss and fur trapping practically eliminated the otter from much of its native range. In an attempt to re-establish this charismatic creature to its former home range, biologists from the University of Tennessee along with state and park officials began a reintroduction program in 1986. Since the first otters were released into Abrams Creek, a number of other otters have been released into other streams throughout Tennessee. With a home range that extends up to 9 miles of stream, the otter population has spread and colonized outside the original stocking locations.

The river otter is the largest member of the weasel family found in the park. Its rich brown fur is short and thick. The body and tail have a torpedo-like shape that can reach up to 4 feet in length. The male otter weighs up to 25 pounds; females are slightly smaller. Strong, webbed feet and a broad, rudder-like tail make them adept swimmers, a skill required when pursuing fish, frogs, and cray-fish—staples in the otter's diet. The otter's ears and nostrils are valved to keep water out during frequent dives underwater.

In the banks of streams, the otter typically builds an underground nest that has a protected underwater entrance hole. In April, female otters raise their litters, normally twins, in these underground homes.

Several physical signs left by otters along waterways show where they are most likely to appear. Slides, which are muddy trails that lead into streams, are telltale signs that otters are using an area. The otter's webbed feet produce five-toed tracks approximately 3 inches in width.

Where To Find River Otters

With the successful expansion of the otter's range, it is possible to find otters along most significant waterways in the park. Although they seem playful, they are not tolerant of disturbances and will seek cover by diving underwater if approached. They are most likely observed by sitting quietly near slow-moving stretches of water, usually during the early morning and late afternoon. The otter is a sociable animal and can be seen moving in groups of two or more. The best places to look for otter are in Abrams Creek, the middle and west fork of the Little Pigeon River, Little River, and Cosby River.

WHITE-TAILED DEER

One of the Great Smoky Mountains' largest and most charismatic species of wildlife is the white-tailed deer (*Odocoileus virginianus*). The deer's big, dark eyes and slender, graceful body make it a favorite animal of park visitors. White-tailed deer are agile creatures capable of running up to 40 mph and leaping up to 20 feet. Its behavior and habitat preferences make it one of the most watchable species of wildlife. The female, or doe, averages 100 pounds, and the male, or buck, weighs about 150 pounds. The buck grows antlers that branch from a single main beam. The animal's colors vary with the seasons; the thick drab-gray coat that protects them during the winter turns to a lighter rusty-red coat for the summer.

Deer tracks are heart-shaped and two-toed, or cloven-hoofed, and usually leave deep impressions. The deer has similar tracks to that of the wild boar, but the boar's tracks are usually found in association with rooting activity.

Bucks polish their antlers in the fall by rubbing them on small trees, leaving signs for watchers to find. They also leave scrapes, which are bare places in the ground marked with its scent to establish territory. The jagged edges that deer leave on branches when feeding is another clue to their presence.

Since deer lack front teeth on the top of their mouths, they leave torn vegetation that is easy to recognize.

The deer raises its tail when alarmed and flashes the white underside. Many times a deer will voice its displeasure at being disturbed by making a loud snort before bounding.

White-tailed deer enter the mating season, or rut, in early November. During this time, bucks spar for dominance using their antlers. Does give birth in April or May. The young fawns rarely venture into the open during the first month; they depend on their spotted coats to camouflage them from predators. Fawns also lack scent, which prevents predators from detecting them. By late June and July, fawns are able to run, defend themselves from predators, and follow their mother to feeding locations.

Also in June, the bucks are in the "velvet" stage; this refers to the velvet-like appearance of the fleshy new antlers the bucks are growing. In order to protect their sensitive antlers, bucks are relatively secretive and solitary at this time. Bucks shed their velvet during the cooler weather of September. The exposed bony growth is recognized as antlers. By this time, fawns have outgrown their spots and look more like adult deer.

The deciduous and pine forests in the park provide protection and food such as acorns and other nuts. Deer spend most of the day bedded in locations where they can watch for predators. With their excellent senses of hearing and smell, they can usually detect park visitors long before they are seen.

Where To Find White-tailed Deer

While common throughout most of the park, deer are uncommon at the higher elevations in the spruce-fir forest; they prefer the meadows and forests of lower elevations. The Cade's Cove area is the best-known area in the park to watch deer. Deer can often be seen grazing in the center pasture of the Cove. They are very tolerant of park visitors who keep their distance. The Sugarlands area is also a good place to see deer along roadsides and in the field beside the visitor center.

On the North Carolina side of the park, Oconaluftee and Cataloochee have meadows and forest edges that attract deer. Cataloochee also has abandoned orchards that deer are unable to resist.

Drivers should always be on the alert for the possibility of deer crossing the road, particularly at night. If a deer is hit, it can do substantial damage to vehicles, cause injury to passengers, and death to the deer.

WILD BOAR

The European wild boar (*Sus scrofa*) is an exotic wildlife species first introduced into western North Carolina around the turn of the century. The species was introduced to provide sport hunting on a private preserve located just south of the park at Hoopers Bald, North Carolina. Descendants of these aggressive omnivores have expanded their range into the Great Smoky Mountains National Park. Being exotic, the wild boar has no natural predators. However, the recently re-introduced red wolf has begun to hunt wild boar. Boar hair has also been found in the scat of coyotes.

Signs of a wild boar are unmistakable and often extensive. Its upturned tusks, which can reach up to 1 foot in length, are used to uproot wildflower bulbs and insect larvae. Foraging wild boars leave a path on the forest floor similar to that of a small bulldozer. They are not selective about their diet. Along with the expected plant material and insect larvae, they eat salamanders and reptiles. Wild boars have also been known to feast on wild turkeys, other birds, and white-tailed deer fawns. Their taste for many of the Smokies' rare plants is even more alarming. "If it is a rare species of orchid," one park service employee said, "the boars probably love it."

The wild boar, measuring up to 3 feet tall at the shoulders and weighing an average of 125 pounds, can be a fierce fighter that exhibits surprising agility for such a large animal. Its hair is coarse and varies from black to gray. The tracks of a wild boar resemble those of the white-tailed deer but are more readily identified when accompanied by signs of rooting and foraging.

The wild boar is a prolific animal that will mate year-round, producing up to twelve piglets per litter and up to two litters per sow a year. Wild boars are the same species as the domestic pig and readily interbred with free-roaming domestic hogs that had been released by nearby farmers to forage before the park was established.

Where To Find Wild Boars

Boars are secretive and as a result are difficult to observe. When seen, they are usually fleeing for cover. Park biologists estimate that less than one thousand boars still inhabit the park area. As a result, it is rare to actually see wild boars in the park.

Look for wild boars at higher elevations such as Newfound Gap, and at lower elevation locations such as Cade's Cove, Tremont, Elkmont, Abrams Creek, and Fontana Reservoir.

GRAY SQUIRREL

The gray squirrel (*Sciurus carolinensis*) is, as its name implies, predominantly gray with a white underside. It weighs about one pound and its bushy, gray tail is used for balance as it scurries through treetops in its high-altitude home.

Foraging on the ground for fallen nuts, the gray squirrel often buries its food for later harvest during cold winter months. It depends on an acute sense of smell to find food caches under as much as 12 inches of snow.

The best way to find gray squirrels is by listening for rustling or crashing noises overhead in trees. Their playful nature and incessant chatter can be distinguished when they are interacting with other squirrels. When threatened, they flatten themselves against a tree on the opposite side of the danger and remain motionless; squirrels depend on their gray fur to provide the perfect camouflage.

The gray squirrel is found mainly in trees that produce nuts, that are staples in the diet of squirrels. These trees are found in the middle and lower deciduous forests of the park, below the 4,500-foot elevation. The gray squirrel's nest is a loosely constructed ball of leaves that can frequently be seen on limbs high in hardwood trees. Unmistakable signs of squirrels are abandoned shells of acorns and other nuts they have dropped to the ground. Often old tree stumps, such as chestnut stumps, provide feeding stations where squirrels can be seen hunched over, eating their nuts. The squirrel's hunched-over posture led to the Cherokee belief that says the condition of individuals afflicted with rheumatism will worsen if they eat the gray squirrel.

Of the five species of arboreal squirrels found in the park, the gray squirrel is the most common. The fox squirrel (*Sciurus niger*) is rare within the park. It weighs almost 3 pounds and is the largest North American species of tree squirrel. The fox squirrel varies in color from black to yellow-gray; it occasionally has a white nose and a large, bushy tail with golden-tipped hairs.

The red squirrel (*Tamiasciurus hudsonicus*) is rusty red, smaller than the gray squirrel, and found at higher elevations. Northern and Southern flying squirrels (*Glaucomys sabrinus* and *Glaucomys volans*) are also found within the park and are easily distinguished from the gray squirrel by their substantially smaller size, large eyes, and almost baggy appearance of their sides as a result of the loose skin folds used for their sailing-type flight.

Where To Find Gray Squirrels

Gray squirrels may be found in Cosby, Greenbrier, Cataloochee, Cade's Cove, and at the Sugarlands visitor center and park headquarters.

It is most often encountered during the early-morning and late-afternoon hours, when it is foraging for food.

EASTERN CHIPMUNK

The Great Smoky Mountains' only species of ground squirrel is the Eastern chipmunk (*Tamias striatus*). To categorize them as a ground squirrel, however, is a bit misleading because the chipmunk also climbs trees in search of food. The name "chipmunk" is thought to be slang for atchitamon, an Algonquian word that refers to the chipmunk's habit of scurrying down a tree head first.

The Eastern chipmunk, a small rusty colored animal with alternating dark and light stripes on its back, weighs a scant 2 to 4 ounces and measures no more than 10 inches from head to tail. It can be distinguished from other squirrel-like animals by its eye-stripe and tail, which it holds erect when scuttling across the forest floor. They are solitary animals that vigorously defend territories from other chipmunks. The sharp "*chup-chup-chup*" call of the chipmunk can be heard throughout the forest.

The chipmunk can be seen actively foraging for food throughout the Smokies. Its diet is primarily composed of vegetable matter such as nuts and berries; however, they are omnivorous and also dine on small insects, snails, and salamanders. It is possible to see chipmunks throughout the year. During harsh winter weather, though, they stay underground, feeding on caches of food. They also go into occasional periods of semi-hibernation or sleep, which slows their metabolism to conserve valuable energy reserves. In the nesting chamber, the female chipmunk raises 2 to 8 young, which are born in May. Chipmunks occasionally raise a second litter in August.

Where To Find Eastern Chipmunks

The chipmunk can be found at all elevations within the park from Abrams Creek to Clingman's Dome. Locally, their population levels vary according to available food sources and desirable habitat. They frequent forested areas, particularly nut-producing deciduous forests, with fallen trees or rocky outcroppings that provide protection from predators. They may be found at Smokemont, Sugarlands, Cosby, and Greenbrier.

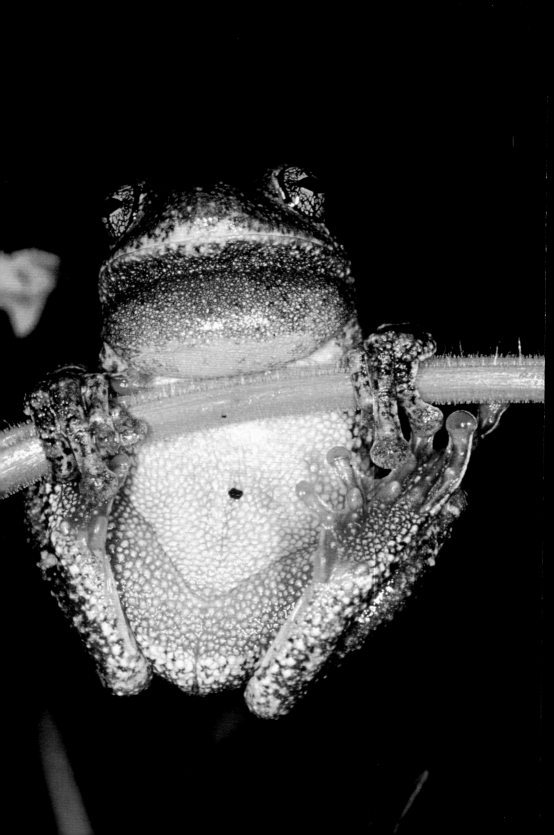

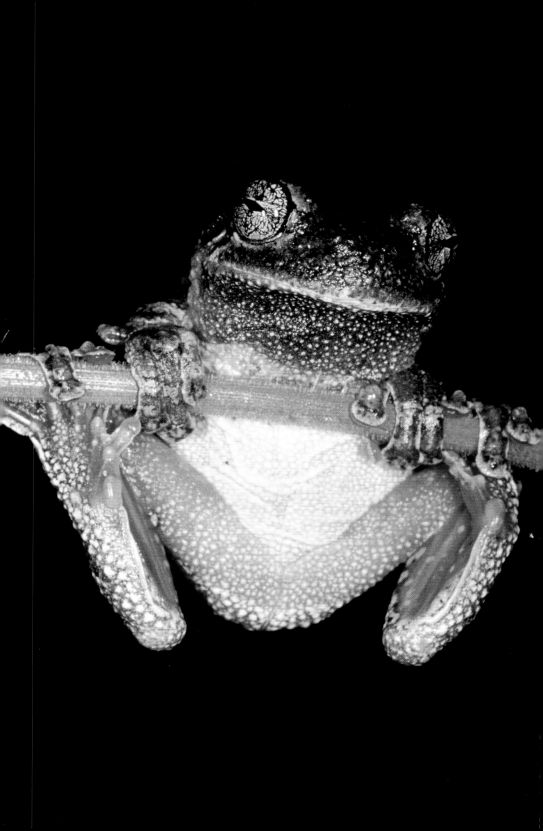

AMPHIBIANS

JORDAN'S SALAMANDER

The woodland salamanders that make up the genus *Plethodon* are a wide-spread and common group that live in the ground litter of the eastern deciduous forest. They are lungless salamanders that breathe primarily through their thin, moist skin and the lining in their mouth. Their colors are extremely variable. It is only in the Smokies, however, that the Jordan group of salamanders (*Plethodon jordani*) have a distinct red cheek patch and, as a result, they are referred to as red-cheeked salamanders. In other areas, this group of salamanders may have red legs or no red at all. Body colors vary from mottled to solid charcoal.

The imitator salamander (*Desmognathus imitator*), another species confined to the Smokies, mimics the red cheek patch of the Jordan salamanders but is a considerably smaller species, averaging between 2 and 4 inches in length.

Although the imitator salamander looks like the Jordan salamander, it lacks the toxic skin secretions that protect the Jordan from predation.

In the spring, this species lays its eggs in small clusters of 10 to 20 eggs under logs and rocks in damp areas. Unlike most salamander eggs, all development of the larvae occurs within the egg, thus lacking any aquatic stage. They emerge from the eggs looking like miniature adults These salamanders dine on small invertebrates and insects including earthworms, crickets and ants.

Where To Find Jordan's Salamanders

Jordan's salamanders are commonly found from the highest elevations at Clingman's Dome to the middle elevations at Chimney's Campground, which is at a 2,800-foot elevation. Salamanders may be found under leaf litter, rock piles, and decomposing logs.

SOUTHERN APPALACHIAN SLIMY SALAMANDER

Identification of salamanders can be confusing and the slimy salamander is no exception. Its physical characteristics include a black body with white spots on the back and sides. The slimy salamander may be relatively large, up to 8 inches in length. In the Smokies, these amphibians may have small red spots on their legs. Some field guides may list the slimy salamander as a single species while others may list the Smokies' equivalent as the Southern Appalachian slimy salamander (*Plethodon teyahalee*). The specific name *teyahalee* refers to Teyahalee Bald, located in the Snowbird Mountains of western North Carolina.

This salamander has a skin gland secretion that leaves a residue so sticky that it can make a predator's jaws stick together. Few predatory animals acquire a taste for these salamanders because of the secretion. For the unsuspecting park visitor who might pick up this salamander, this residue will wear off.

Reproduction in the Southern Appalachian is like other woodland salamanders in that it lacks an aquatic stage.

Because of their biological diversity, more than twenty different species of salamanders call the Great Smoky Mountains home. Their habitats range from Abrams Creek (only 857 feet in elevation) to Clingman's Dome (6,643 feet), the highest point in the park. Salamanders represent an ancient group of amphibians that evolved along with the ancient Southern Appalachian mountains of the Smokies.

Where To Find Southern Appalachian Slimy Salamanders

Slimy salamanders may be seen throughout the park in moist, forested areas with elevations up to 5,500 feet, like Cade's Cove.

RED-SPOTTED NEWT

The life cycle stages of the red-spotted newt (*Notophthalmus viridescens viridescens*) can be easily observed in the Great Smoky Mountains.

In March, adult newts congregate in still pools of water where they lay their eggs and attach them singly to aquatic vegetation. Some female newts take up to one week to lay three to four hundred eggs. After incubating for up to 8 weeks, the newly hatched newts emerge. They are green, measure less than 1/2 inch in length, and have flattened tails and external, branched gills.

About three months after hatching, the aquatic life of juvenile newts temporarily ends with their emergence as the orange-colored eft—a juvenile stage of the newt's life. For the next one to three years, the eft will lead a terrestrial life on the Smokies' moist forest floor. The brilliant orange color is thought to be a warning to potential predators. If the rough, dry skin of the eft is bruised, it releases a toxic secretion distasteful to predators such as weasels and skunks. This defense mechanism may explain why the red-spotted salamander, unlike most other salamander species, can be seen during the daylight; particularly during warm summer rains. Autumn marks a migration of efts moving to pools of water to complete their metamorphosis into adult newts. Emerging from subterranean cover in late winter, adult newts start the process over again.

Adult newts are olive-green in color with red spots. The males have a wide, flattened tail fin and black horny growths that appear during the mating season. Males use these growths to improve their grasp on the females. Male newts are also a darker shade of green than the female. The female newts lack flattened tails and horny growths.

Where To Find Red-spotted Newts

The red-spotted newt lives at lower and middle elevations where suitable breeding pools are found. The bright orange eft often can be found on moist forest floors after summer rains. From January through March, adult newts are around the edges of water, such as in limestone sinks in Cade's Cove, and around slow-moving stretches of low-elevation streams.

GRAY TREEFROG

Two species of gray treefrogs are found in the Great Smoky Mountains. Although practically impossible to distinguish by physical characteristics, the Cope's gray treefrog (*Hyla chrysoscelis*) and the common gray treefrog (*Hyla versicolor*) can be identified by their song. Both species' song is a musical trill. The song of the Cope's gray treefrog, however, is higher and more rapid than the common gray treefrog's. Since their ranges overlap in many areas, you may hear both at the same time.

The physical characteristics and behavior of both species are practically identical. Although not as warty as toads, gray treefrogs have rough warty skin with blotchy gray-green patterns that provide camouflage in the deciduous hardwood forest. The gray treefrog measures up to 2 inches in length. Hidden beneath the hind legs is a brilliant patch of orange color. They possess the large toe pads characteristic in treefrogs, which allow them to cling to most surfaces. Males can be identified by their dark, almost black throats. The females have light-colored throats.

When at rest, the treefrog folds its front legs under its chin and compresses its body flat to whatever it is clinging to. This eliminates the frog's shadow and disguises it from potential predators.

The gray treefrog has a unique method of surviving the winter months. The frogs accumulate large amounts of glycerol, an antifreeze, in their cells. Studies have shown that they can withstand several days in below-freezing temperatures with as much as 40 percent of their body water frozen. The normally damaging effects of cellular ice crystals appear to have minimal effects on the frog, even with repeated thawing and freezing.

Where To Find Gray Treefrogs

During their mating season from April to June, the gray treefrog is most commonly observed in or near small breeding pools at lower elevations, such as Cataloochee and Sugarlands. During other times of the year, they rarely vocalize and return to an arboreal life that makes them difficult to find. These treefrogs are not limited to lower elevations, however, and have been found as high as Gregory Bald, which is almost 5,000 feet.

REPTILES

NORTHERN FENCE LIZARD

Hikers in the Great Smoky Mountains are most often made aware of the presence of the Northern fence lizard (*Sceloporus undulatus hyacinthinus*), or "swift"
as it is known locally, by the sound of the lizard scurrying to find refuge on the
opposite side of a nearby tree. Its light and dark-gray coloration blends perfect-
ly with the dry oak and pine woodlands that it prefers. This 4- to 7-inch-long
lizard is usually found below elevations of 3,000 feet; however, it has been found
as high as High Rocks, which is 5,188 feet.

The male Northern fence lizard has a bright blue chin and flanks. The female
is a more mottled-gray color and lacks the brilliant blue underparts. The male
fence lizard uses its coloring to defend its territory. It conceals its blue body parts
by flattening itself against a tree or fence post and flashes the blue parts by bob-
bing up and down; this flashing effect makes the lizard's display more obvious.

The female fence lizard also possesses a yellow underside on its tail. Northern fence lizards lay groups of 3 to 13 eggs that hatch in summer.

This lizard's camouflaging gray coloration conceals it from predators such as bobcats and long-tailed weasels. The color also aids the lizard in its daytime pursuit of moths and other insects on which it feeds, found on the bark of trees.

Where To Find Northern Fence Lizards

The northern fence lizard can be found at most of the trailheads where old fencing, rock piles, or other structures provide cover for the lizard. These lizards may be found in Cade's Cove, Oconaluftee, and Cataloochee.

NORTHERN COPPERHEAD

The Great Smoky Mountains' master of camouflage is the Northern copperhead (*Agkistrodon contortix mokesen*). The copperhead has alternating hourglass-shaped bands of rust or copper and tan. Its coloration enables it to blend with its surroundings—fallen deciduous tree leaves—and makes the snake almost invisible.

Like the timber rattler (*Crotalus horridus*), the copperhead is a venomous pit viper. The copperhead is smaller than the timber rattler, rarely exceeding 42 inches in length. Several nonvenomous snakes mimic the appearance of the copperhead but lack the hourglass-shaped markings. The corn, or red rat, snake (*Elaphe guttata guttata*) looks similar to the copperhead, but is a nonvenomous constrictor. It has a much smaller body shape and a narrower, less triangular head.

Surprisingly, in the Smokies, much of the copperhead's diet is composed of insects, especially cicadas. Copperheads will, however, feed on small mammals, reptiles, and birds.

61

During warm days in the spring and fall, these snakes can be seen basking in the sun near fallen logs and rocky outcroppings. Copperheads become mostly nocturnal during the summer months and can occasionally be seen at night soaking up residual heat from the pavement of park roads. Winter months signal the copperhead's return to dens to wait for warm weather to return.

Where To Find Northern Copperheads

The Northern copperhead is considered an uncommon snake in the park; it is rarely found above 2,500 feet in elevation and prefers the deciduous forests of the lower elevations. Copperheads may be found in the Rich Mountain–Cade's Cove section of the park.

TIMBER RATTLESNAKE

The timber rattlesnake (*Crotalus horridus*), as the name implies, has distinctive rattles on its tail that produces a buzzing noise when the snake is alarmed. A new rattle is added each time the snake sheds its skin, usually two to four times per year. The number of rattles does not necessarily tell the age of a rattlesnake because rattles routinely break.

The skin color of this pit viper varies from black to cream or yellow. The timber rattlesnake also has a dark V-shaped pattern on its back with a solid black tail. The length of some timber rattlesnakes can exceed 5 feet, but 3 feet is more common.

Pit vipers possess a heat-sensitive pit located between the eye and the nostril. Characteristics of this group of snakes include an elliptical or cat-like pupil; stout, heavy body shapes; and heads that are clearly wider than the necks.

The venom of pit vipers digestively attacks muscle tissue. Hollow fangs inject venom into the bloodstream of the snake's victims, such as mice and voles, quickly killing the prey.

If you find a timber rattler or copperhead, follow a few rules to make your encounter safe. Remember that a pit viper cannot strike out more than one-half of its body length. For example, if you stay more than 2 feet away from a 4-foot long snake, the animal will not be able to reach you. Give the snake the needed room. Don't harass it. Most venomous snakebites in Tennessee parks have occurred as a result of someone trying to handle or catch a snake. It is important to stay on designated trails, because rattlesnakes do not hunt on trails with heavy foot traffic. Snakes are most often encountered when walking off trails or along rocky outcroppings and stream beds.

Where To Find Timber Rattlesnakes

Timber rattlesnakes may be found at all elevations around rock piles and on grassy balds throughout the park. They have been recorded at elevations as high as 6,600 feet on Mount Guyot.

BIRDS

EASTERN SCREECH OWL

The mournful, whinnying call of the Eastern screech owl (*Otus asio*) sounds as though it should be coming from a much larger bird. Only 10 inches tall, this diminutive owl has a haunting voice. Two mottled color phases of screech owl are found in the park. Across the eastern United States, the red phase is more common in the southern portions of the screech owl's range; the gray phase is more common in the north. This trend holds true in the Smokies with the red phase outnumbering the gray phase four to one. As with most nocturnal owls, the screech owl has large yellow eyes. Distinctive ear tufts can been seen on the tops of their heads.

Screech owls are cavity nesters laying between 2 to 7 pure white eggs that hatch after 26 days. Nesting occurs in the spring of the year.

The screech owl is a fearless nocturnal hunter that feeds primarily on small mammals, such as deer mice, but is able to kill birds larger than itself, such as the ruffed grouse. These owls, which often hunt near small streams, will also dine on crayfish. During certain times of the year, abundant insects provide a substantial portion of their diet. Their propensity to hunt small birds is evident by the noisy, mobbing reaction of songbirds to the call of the screech owl.

When encountered during daylight hours, screech owls hoping to avoid detection remain motionless and seem to squint, presumably to hide the bright yellow of their eyes.

Where To Find Eastern Screech Owls

Eastern screech owls are often seen in the hollow cavities of trees where they nest. They can be attracted at night by imitating their tremulous call. Eastern screech owls may be found in open woodlands in elevations below 4,000 feet. The forests around Oconaluftee, Cataloochee, and Sugarlands are good areas to attempt nighttime calling.

BARRED OWL

The barred owl (*Strix varia*) is the most day-active, or diurnal, owl species found in the Great Smoky Mountains. Even during the daylight hours, the owl's echoing call of *"Who cooks for you? Who cooks for you all?"* can be heard throughout the park. The single *"hooo-aaw"* call of this owl is occasionally heard as a single, extended and descending vocalization; it is this call that gives the barred owl the common nickname of "hoot owl." Both sexes of barred owls indulge in these spectacular vocalizations. The female has a slightly higher pitched voice than the male. They are gregarious birds that are attracted to the calls or the imitations of other barred owls. When several owls congregate, the hooting calls degenerate into raucous screams that sound more monkey-like than bird-like. Vocalizations can be heard at all times of the year. The owl's calls can be easily imitated and is effective in attracting owls.

In the spring, barred owls lay 2 to 3 white eggs in cavity nests or abandoned hawk nests. Incubation lasts around 30 days.

The barred owl lacks the large ear tufts found on the great horned owl, the only other large, dark-colored owl found in the park. The barred owl has dark-brown eyes that aid its diurnal habits. The feathers are a soft, mottled brown with light and dark barring on its chest. The feathers of owls have soft edges designed for silent flight and result in a fluffy appearance. The female owl, as with most predatory birds, is larger than the male.

Mice and other small mammals make up the majority of the barred owl's diet, but these birds have also been known to catch fish. Barred owls often have feeding nests, or roosts, which they use to devour and digest captured meals. Unable to completely digest the bones, feathers, and fur of its prey, the owl regurgitates pellets that can be found below these roosts. These pellets provide a detailed menu of the owl's food preferences.

Where To Find Barred Owls

Barred owls prefer low-elevation wetland areas and streamsides, and the higher-elevation spruce-fir forests. Barred owls can be found in the spruce-fir forests of Mount LeConte, Clingman's Dome, and Newfound Gap and at lower elevations, such as Oconaluftee and Cade's Cove.

WILD TURKEY

The wild turkey (*Meleagris gallopavo*) is the Great Smoky Mountains' largest species of bird. It is much more streamlined than the barnyard turkey. The male wild turkey, or gobbler, can weigh over 20 pounds but averages around 16 pounds; they can stand almost 4 feet tall. Hen turkeys, which are smaller, weigh just under 10 pounds and stand 3 feet tall.

Hens lack the leg spurs and long beard that the male possesses. The male's beard looks like a long tuft of horse hair protruding from the chest; it is actually modified feathers that can reach a length of 1 foot or more. Hens may also possess beards, but these rarely exceed 3 inches. Wild turkey feathers have a dark-bronze iridescence that looks almost black from a distance. The hen's color is slightly lighter. The regal appearance of the wild turkey prompted Ben Franklin to choose this bird, rather than the bald eagle, as the national symbol.

Adult birds feed mainly on the nuts of trees such as oaks. The signs of foraging turkeys are unmistakable because they scratch leaf litter away in search of acorns. These foraging signs differ from those of the wild boar which literally digs into the ground with its tusks. Turkey tracks can sometimes be seen in muddy spots along trails. The large tracks measure 3 or more inches in width and display four long toes.

Turkeys perform elaborate courtship rituals in the late winter and spring. Male birds strut and display their rusty-colored, broad tail feathers. Many times during courtship, the male's bare head will change from bright red to blue. During this time of year, turkeys are very vocal with the "gobbling" call of the male bird being heard up to a mile away. Male turkeys collect a harem of 5 to 6 hens that stay with him until all the eggs are laid.

Turkeys normally roost high in hardwood trees over streams or other bodies of water. Nests are built in wooded areas on the ground usually well concealed by vegetation. About 28 days after being laid, the 10 to 13 eggs hatch. Young turkeys are precocious. They are capable of feeding themselves and making short flights one week after hatching. Hens prefer to nest in fields and forest edges because of the large numbers of insects upon which young turkeys feed. As these birds mature, they occasionally join other hens with their broods to form large flocks that will stay together through the next mating season.

Where To Find Wild Turkeys

The wild turkey is an uncommon, permanent resident that can be found at all elevations in the park, although it was once considered a rare sighting in the southern Appalachians. One of the most commonly seen flocks of wild turkeys live in Cade's Cove. Occasionally, these birds can be seen in the pastures of the Cove. They are most often spotted at the edge of fields and in the forests, rarely venturing into the center of large fields. These secretive birds are most often detected during the early and late hours of the day. In the Cove, turkeys are most often seen near the Methodist church and the Hyatt Lane area.

RED-WINGED BLACKBIRD

The mechanical, high-pitched *"o-ka-lee"* call of the red-winged blackbird (*Agelaius phoeniceus*) is a song of rebirth in the marsh and signals the end of winter's lean season. The red-winged blackbird, which is sometimes considered an exclusively marsh-nesting animal, can be found near most bodies of water and also in upland fields. The male is glossy black with bright red patches, or epaulets, on the shoulders. The female is drab and inconspicuous with an appearance much like that of a large sparrow.

The red-winged blackbird has several interesting territorial displays. The males arrive on the breeding grounds several weeks before the females in order to establish territories. They select perches within their territory to sing and display their brilliant wing patches. Subordinate male birds outside their established territories will not display the bright red wing patches. The male red-winged blackbirds also make wide low-level flights within their territories to reveal their epaulets. The displays are used to warn other males to stay away and to attract mates.

Usually three females will nest in the territory of a single male. Nesting pairs of birds may raise up to three broods, with three to five pale-blue eggs in each brood. The nests, which are made from woven grasses and other vegetation, are suspended in reeds and branches.

Red-winged blackbirds join cowbirds, starlings, grackles, and other black-birds during the fall and spring in massive migration flights. These large flocks seek out fields and marshes with abundant food sources such as grain, seeds, and insects.

Where To Find Red-winged Blackbirds

Red-winged blackbirds may be found near streams and pastures in Cade's Cove, Oconaluftee, Cataloochee, and Abrams Creek.

COMMON RAVEN

The quintessential symbol of wilderness in the East is the common raven (*Corvus corax*). This crow-like bird can be found soaring the thermal updrafts of some of the highest and most secluded points in the Appalachian Mountains. The raven is the largest of North America's passerines.

The crow-like appearance of the raven is deceiving because the raven possesses several differences from the common crow. While the raven is completely black like the crow, its bill is heavier and shielded by hair-like feathers; its neck feathers give it a bearded appearance. The raven's tail is longer and more wedge-shaped than the crow's tail. The raven also has a wingspan approximately 6 inches wider than that of the crow.

The ranges of the two birds rarely overlap, but when they do, the smaller crow often mobs and harasses the raven much like it would a hawk or an owl. The call of the raven is an assortment of croaks except in immature birds that "caw" like crows. The raven's flight pattern includes typically slow, heavy wing-beats that exploit the winds and thermal drafts of its mountain home. The aerial courtship of the raven includes soaring in circles much like that of the red-tailed hawk.

The raven is a scavenging feeder that is said to mate for life. Large nests constructed near the tops of coniferous trees or on rocky ledges often contain 4 to 7 greenish eggs with brown spots.

Where To Find Common Ravens

In the Great Smoky Mountains, common ravens prefer the balds and forests found at elevations above 5,000 feet. These areas are dominated by red spruce and Fraser fir trees, forming what is often referred to as the Canadian life zone.

This bird can be found at the Alum Cave Bluffs Trail, the Appalachian Trail near the spruce-fir forests of Mount LeConte, along the Appalachian Trail at the Tennessee-North Carolina border, Newfound Gap and the Newfound Gap parking area, and the entire length of the Clingman's Dome Road. It also occasionally ventures into Cade's Cove.

BELTED KINGFISHER

Visitors to many of the streams in the Great Smoky Mountains are often treated to the feeding routine of one of the park's most vociferous residents, the belted kingfisher (*Ceryle alcyon*). The kingfisher can be easily recognized in flight by its deep, swooping wing-beats that lead it on an almost roller-coaster-like flight pattern. It often calls in flight while traveling the waterways; frequently, the rapid, ratchet-like call is heard long before the bird is seen. When feeding, the kingfisher hovers above the water and then dives headfirst, catching small fish in its beak. The belted kingfisher is a blue-jay-sized bird that measures 12 inches long.

Unlike most other bird species, the female belted kingfisher is more colorful than the male; she possesses a rusty-colored belly band the male lacks. The robust body shape of both sexes is gray-blue with white bands around the belly and neck. The head is broad and crested, and the beak is long and stout.

The kingfishers' nest-making process is a labor-intensive activity. With its stout bill, it digs holes in steep dirt banks along the side of streams. Nesting chambers may be located more than 1 foot deep in these underground nests where it lays 5 to 8 glossy white eggs.

Where To Find Belted Kingfishers

The belted kingfisher is most often seen along major streams and lakes in the park. They may also be found around Abrams Creek, Fontana Lake, the Little River Road, and the Little Pigeon River in Greenbrier.

RED-TAILED HAWK

Named for its rusty-red tail, the red-tailed hawk (*Buteo jamaicensis*) is the park's most common buteo. Buteos are birds of prey that have broad wings and a tail that they use for soaring in wide circles. This group of birds also has exceptional eyesight; it has been said that if the hawk could read, it could read a newspaper from 100 yards away.

Juvenile red-tail hawks can be seen in the late summer. They are the size of the adult but lack the red tail. Their tails are lighter gray and sometimes banded; they grow red tails at two years of age. Juvenile red-tails are also commonly lighter in color and more mottled; they lack the uniform dark-brown back of adult birds. Red-tails have a streaked, brown band across their belly that is a diagnostic field mark.

The sexes of this species are similar in appearance, although the female bird is visibly larger than the male and has a wingspan of up to 4 feet wide (compared to the male's slightly smaller 3-1/2 feet width).

The call of the red-tailed hawk is a piercing scream that sounds defiant and free. Its call is often used in movies to establish a wild and untamed setting.

Red-tailed hawks are uncommon, year-round residents that nest in the park. Nests are made of sticks. Soaring adult birds can be a clue to the location of their nests which, though large, are difficult to find. Red-tails lay 2 to 3 brown-splotched eggs that hatch 30 days later. Males bring food to the nesting female during incubation.

Where To Find Red-tailed Hawks

Fall populations often rise as northern red-tailed hawks migrate south in search of better food sources. These birds prefer open fields and woodland edges; they are often seen soaring overhead or perched in trees in Cade's Cove, Cataloochee, Oconaluftee, and at Look Rock on the Foothills Parkway.

EASTERN BLUEBIRD

There is a certain magnetism to the Eastern bluebird (*Sialia sialis*). The brilliant-blue male is a symbol—a promise—of spring. This bird often evokes a more personal attachment when it is observed in bluebird boxes next to houses. Observing fledgling bluebirds as they flit from fence post to fence post along Hyatt Lane near Cade's Cove makes a trip to the Smokies all the more memorable.

Both the male and female bluebird have bluish backs with rusty breasts; however, the female bird, like immature bluebirds, is a little more drab. The back of the male Eastern bluebird is one of nature's most brilliant hues of blue. In the Smokies, there are three other "blue" bird species that can be easily distinguished from the Eastern bluebird. The blue jay (*Cyanocitta cristata*) has a crested-head and is much larger. The indigo bunting (*Passerina cyanea*) and the blue grosbeak (*Guiraca caerulea*) are blue but lack the rusty-colored breast of the bluebird.

The call of the Eastern bluebird is a soft musical *"tur-a-wee"* or *"chur-wee"* with scattered chatter. The bluebird can be seen singing from perches within the established nesting territories of mating pairs.

Interestingly, the male bluebird defends the territory, which is usually open fields and forest edges, from other male bluebirds and the female defends the territory from other females. Territories are aggressively defended in the fall in order to protect the nesting hollows used to shelter the bluebird family from harsh Appalachian winters. During cold winter nights, bluebird families conserve warmth by congregating in hollow trees and old nesting sites.

Where To Find Eastern Bluebirds

The Eastern bluebird is a fairly common year-round resident of the park. It is often found perched on fence posts in Cade's Cove and at the edge of open fields and grassy areas at Oconaluftee and Sugarlands.

TURKEY VULTURE

Turkey vultures (*Cathartes aura*) are the cleanup crew in the Great Smoky Mountains because they dine on carrion, or dead animals. It is a task for which the vulture is well equipped; it has a featherless head that does not require preening, thus reducing the chances of accumulating dirt and bacteria.

The turkey vulture is one of two species of vultures found in the park. The black vulture (*Coragyps atratus*) frequents many of the same areas as the turkey vulture. Turkey vultures have black bodies with red, fleshy heads and wingspans that reach up to 6 feet in width, which is more than 1-1/2 feet wider than black vultures. Black vultures have black, fleshy heads.

The underwings of the turkey vulture are black and silvery in flight and its tail feathers are long and narrow. Its flight pattern is deep and labored; these birds rarely flap their wings and use thermal drafts to stay in the air. The underwing tips of the black vulture in flight are white, and it has a short, squared tail. Their flight pattern depends more on strong wing-beats and less on updrafts.

While both species dine primarily on carrion, the hunting techniques of these two vultures also differ. The turkey vulture depends on an acute sense of smell to detect odors while soaring aloft. The black vulture depends primarily on its eye-sight to locate food; but because it lacks an acute sense of smell, it may depend on the turkey vulture to lead it to food. The black vulture, a much more aggressive bird, will kill weak or sick animals for food.

Turkey vultures nest on high cliffs and rocky outcroppings. They lay 2 eggs on the bare ground.

Where To Find Turkey Vultures

Turkey vultures may be seen soaring on thermals above most elevations in the park. Look Rock on the Foothills Parkway is a good place to watch vultures soaring in the valley below. Occasionally they can also be seen gathered in roosting flocks in Cade's Cove.

GALLERY

STRIPED SKUNK

One of mother nature's most recogniz-able animals is the skunk. Two species are found within the park. The striped skunk (*Mephitis mephitis*) is black and has two wide white bands or stripes that run from the top of its head to its tail. Even in the dark, the gait of the striped skunk is unmistakable. A shuffling, almost waddling stride is proof that the skunk is rarely in a hurry. The Eastern spotted skunk (*Spilogale putoriu*), also found in the park, is smaller (2 to 3 pounds) and less common than the striped skunk, which weighs 6 to 14 pounds. The spotted skunk has several broken white lines or spots and a characteristic white tip on its tail.

The bold coloration and flag-like tail of the striped skunk is a signal to all who might pose a threat to stay clear. The odor for which skunks are known is an oily musk, which the animal sprays from its anal glands when it feels threatened. Normally, a skunk sends a warning when it is about to spray by lifting its tail and stamping its feet. However, if a skunk is surprised, it can spray immediately. The scent of the musk can travel up to a mile away and is extremely persistent. If sprayed in the eyes of a potential predator, the musk can cause temporary blindness.

Skunks are omnivorous; they will eat vegetable matter and other animals. It is this eating habit that frequently brings them to campgrounds and picnic areas searching for scraps that park visitors might have left. Skunks can be interesting to watch, but because they can be carriers of the rabies virus they should be given space. The great horned owl is considered the only serious predator of skunks in the park.

The striped skunk is a common resident that is normally found below 5,200 feet elevation. Look for them around most park campgrounds, lowland streams, field edges, and picnic areas, such as in Cade's Cove.

DEER MOUSE

The deer mouse (*Peromyscus maniculatus*) is one of the Great Smoky Mountains' most common mammals. They are ubiquitous, inhabiting all patches of the park that provide enough seed for food and cover from predators. They are prolific, and may produce as many as six young per litter and up to four litters per year. A strong population of deer mice is essential because these animals are a staple food in the diet of almost every carnivore and omnivore found in the park.

The deer mouse is rusty-brown to gray in color with a white belly. These small animals weigh from 1/2 to 1 ounce and measure from 5 to 9 inches in length from head to tail.

The deer mouse closely resembles the white-footed mouse (*Peromyscus leucopus*), which is often found in the same locations as deer mice. The tail length and coloration are the best field identification characteristics that separate these two species. The deer mouse has been called the long-tailed deer mouse in the past. Its long tail, which measures up to 5 inches in length, is dark on top and white on the bottom. The tail of the white-footed mouse is shorter, less than 4 inches, and lacks the distinct bicoloration of the deer mouse's tail.

The deer mouse, a distinctly northern and western species, has a range that extends down the spine of the Appalachian Mountains. These animals prefer cooler temperatures. Their range in the park extends from below the 2,000-foot elevation to above 6,000 feet.

Deer mice may be found at Mount LeConte, Newfound Gap, Clingman's Dome, and other high-elevation locations.

RED SQUIRREL

The red squirrel (*Tamiasciurus hudsonicus*) is generally considered a northern forest animal; however, it reaches the southeastern limit of its range just south of the park in northern Georgia. It is a fairly common resident of the park. It prefers the evergreen spruce-fir forest at high elevations during summer months, and Canadian hemlock stands during winter months.

Weighing a scant 5 to 9 ounces, the red squirrel is substantially smaller than the gray and fox squirrels that are also found in the park. It is rusty-red to reddish-gray in color with a white belly. During the summer months, a distinct black line separates its white belly from its reddish back.

Piles of evergreen cones that have been stripped of their seeds are an indication the red squirrel has been present. Nests can be found in hollows in stumps and trees or in coniferous trees. The red squirrel makes round nests from stripped and shredded bark and assorted herbaceous vegetation. In addition to evergreen cones, the red squirrel also eats nuts, berries, and even mushrooms. Like the gray squirrel, it stores food caches underground.

The red squirrel can be found at higher elevations in the park in northern hardwood stands, hemlock groves, and in the spruce-fir forest. They have been seen at lower elevations near the park headquarters and Sugarlands. Look for them at the Clingman's Dome parking lot and trail, Newfound Gap, Mount LeConte, and along the Alum Cave Bluff Trail.

WOOD FROG

Preferring to spend most of the year on the moist forest floor, the habits of the wood frog (*Rana sylvatica*) are more toad-like than other frogs' found in the park. The wood frog is an early egg layer; it sometimes lays its eggs before all winter ice has melted. Many wood frogs make a very brief appearance at the water's edge for a short frenzied courtship. They quickly lay their eggs and then return to the forest.

Although the wood frog frequents areas usually inhabited by toads, there are several differences between these frogs and toads. The wood frog belongs to a group of animals that include toads called "anurans," which means "without a tail." The frog's skin is moist and fairly smooth, while the toad's skin is dry and warty. The frog's legs are much longer in comparison to that of a toad. Wood frogs lay their eggs in a round mass whereas toads lay their eggs in strings.

The color of the wood frog varies from pink to brown to almost black; however, a dark eye patch extending from the nostrils toward the front legs is visible. The male frog is usually darker, almost black, during the mating season and smaller than the female.

While the wood frog has been found in middle elevations up to 3,900 feet, it prefers lower elevations below 2,500 feet. During winter months, wood frogs burrow under leaves on the forest floor; they are protected from freezing conditions by a sort of vascular antifreeze that prevents damage to cells that are exposed to freezing temperatures. In January and February, the quack-like song is a signal to help locate them around the margin of sinkhole ponds and wet areas found in Oconaluftee, Cade's Cove, and Cataloochee, especially on mild, rainy nights. They can be found in forested areas during spring and summer months.

AMERICAN TOAD

In March the incessant trill of the male American toad (*Bufo americanus americanus*) signals the end of winter and the birth of another spring. This harbinger of spring is a common resident of the park.

The American toad possesses the warty, dry skin and short hind legs that are typical of toads. Within the park, only Fowler's toad (*Bufo woodhousii fowleri*) looks similar to the American toad. The dark spots on the back distinguish the two species: American toads have one or two warts per spot as opposed to the Fowler's toad that may have up to seven warts per spot. The color of the American toad varies from dark brown to a rusty-red. The two large warts on the backs of these frogs are called parotid glands and are used for defensive purposes. These glands release a toxic secretion when the toad feels threatened. The predator may foam at the mouth or become ill if it ingests too much toxin.

On the night of the first mild spring rains in March, large numbers of toads emerge from their underground winter burrows. The falling barometric pressure and the related rains in the spring are thought to provide the stimulus for this mass exodus from hibernation. Thousands of toads appear at the edges of small pools and ponds and trigger breeding.

The toad's eggs are laid in strings attached to substrates on the bottom of small pools of water. These eggs hatch into tiny immature toads, often called tadpoles or pollywogs. In 3 to 4 weeks, the metamorphosis from a wiggling aquatic creature with a tail to a miniature toad is complete.

American toads have been recorded at elevations above 5,000 feet; however, these animals prefer the lower and middle elevations within the park. They can be seen in Cade's Cove, Sugarlands, Cataloochee, and Oconaluftee at night after warm spring rains. At night they can be found around light sources that attract nocturnal insects.

LONGTAIL SALAMANDER

The longtail salamander (*Eurycea longicauda longicauda*), a fairly common amphibian in the park, seeks shelter under rotting logs, rocks, near streams, and occasionally in caves. This salamander is a yellowish-orange in color. It has black spots on its body, and herring-bone shaped black blotches along its tail.

The tail produces a distasteful secretion, and is used as a defense mechanism. When threatened, the salamander will lift its tail above its body. This ensures that the tail is the first body part the predator will attack; the bad taste makes the predator look elsewhere for more palatable prey. If the tail is lost or damaged during the attack, the salamander will grow a new one.

On warm rainy nights, longtail salamanders occasionally can be seen searching the forest floor for small insects. Eggs are laid during the winter months in underground openings near springs and streams.

The state line between North Carolina and Tennessee is the eastern limit in the park of this salamander's range. Longtail salamanders are found in the lower elevations on the Tennessee side of the park at Cade's Cove, Sugarlands, and Abrams Creek.

SPOTTED SALAMANDER

Although spotted salamanders (*Ambystoma maculatum*) are rarely seen outside the breeding season, large numbers appear when heavy, late winter rains trigger the mating urge. Spotted salamanders are classified as mole salamanders and, as the name implies, they spend most of their life underground dining on earthworms and other subterranean denizens. The spotted salamander is one of the largest terrestrial salamanders found in the park, growing up to 8 inches in length. It is black with yellow spots. The belly is a lighter slate-gray color without spots.

The spotted salamander is found only at the lowest elevations (below 2,200 feet) on the Tennessee side of the park. It can be found in January and February in moist forest areas near sinkhole pools in Laurel Creek near Cade's Cove, Sugarlands, Elkmont, and Greenbrier. They may share breeding pools with marbled salamanders and wood frogs. At other times during the year, the spotted salamander retreats under rotting logs in the forest floor.

TUFTED TITMOUSE

Known as a common visitor to household bird feeders, the tufted titmouse (*Parus bicolor*) is a common, permanent resident of the Great Smoky Mountains. Named for the tufted crest on its head, the titmouse has a gray body with rusty-tinted flanks and is 4 to 5 inches long.

Nesting pairs of titmice aggressively defend territories during the spring nesting season. Their nests are found in natural cavities and are constructed of a variety of materials including moss, bark, animal hair, and even snake skin. During the fall and winter months, tufted titmice often congregate in flocks with parents and offspring of the past nesting season. They can also be found foraging for food in mixed flocks of chickadees, small woodpeckers, and nuthatches.

The song of the tufted titmouse is a repetitive series of whistled notes saying *"peter, peter, peter."* Being a somewhat gregarious bird, titmice often can be heard scolding each other, vocalizing assorted, high-pitched nasal wheezes.

The tufted titmouse is not common in the higher elevations in the park. Below the 5,000 feet elevation, however, they are considered a common year-round resident. Look for them in the Cosby, Roaring Fork, Sugarlands, Oconaluftee, and Cataloochee sections of the park.

BARN SWALLOW

The barn swallow (*Hirundo rustica*) has a dark navy-colored back and rusty-colored breast. The most easily identified field sign of this bird is its deeply forked tail. While other swallow species have notched tails, the barn swallow is North America's only swallow with an inverted V-shaped notched tail. The barn swallow is 6 to 8 inches long.

In flight, the barn swallow is one of the Great Smoky Mountains' most acrobatic birds. These birds often can be found in concentrations, swooping low over water and fields and dipping and diving for airborne insects. Their gregarious nature allows them to feed with other species of swallows and chimney swifts. Barn swallows are social nesters and may nest in the same location in old barns and structures as other swallows. The mud nests lined with feathers are attached to walls and on the top of beams in locations protected from the weather.

Barn swallows can be found near historic structures and feeding in nearby fields in Cade's Cove, Oconaluftee, and Cataloochee. They can also be seen feeding on insects near the surface of the water of Fontana Reservoir.

AMERICAN GOLDFINCH

Sometimes referred to as wild canaries because of the male's brilliant yellow summer plumage, the American goldfinch (*Carduelis tristis*) is a fairly common permanent resident of the Great Smoky Mountains National Park. The colorful male goldfinch has a bright yellow body that contrasts with a solid black cap on its head and black-and-white wings and tail. Female goldfinches are also yellow, but are generally duller in color and lack the black cap. During the winter, both the male and female display a dull-gray plumage similar to the female's summer plumage. They are about 5 inches long.

The goldfinch is the latest-nesting bird species in the park; it nests from July into September. Because the bird utilizes the thistle down as a nest lining, the nesting season of the goldfinch coincides with the maturation of thistle seeds. These birds feed on thistle and dandelion seeds during the summer months; during the winter months, goldenrod, ragweed, and thistle plants attract flocks of up to a hundred foraging goldfinches.

The flight of the American goldfinch is a good identifying characteristic. Their flight is undulating, similar to the rhythm of a roller coaster. They flap their wings several times and then coast for a brief moment before starting the sequence over again. This flight is thought to be an energy-conservation strategy.

The song of the goldfinch is a high, sweet *"per-chik-o-ree,"* but excited chips and twitters are also heard when a flock of them are nearby. They chatter noticeably in flight.

Although found at locations throughout the park, most commonly below 4,500 feet in elevation, the fields around Cade's Cove and the Sugarlands area are some of the best locations to find the American goldfinch.

CAROLINA CHICKADEE

No southern forest would be complete without the high-pitched *"chickadee-dee-dee"* song that gives the Carolina chickadee (*Parus carolinensis*) its name. With a black cap and chin, this small gray-and-black bird is a frequent visitor to bird feeders and is a common year-round resident of the Great Smoky Mountains.

The black-capped chickadee is a close relative of the Carolina chickadee and looks very similar to it. Location is one of the best ways to distinguish these two birds. The black-capped chickadee is a northerly species that reaches the southern limit of its nesting range in the park. During the summer months, black-caps prefer to stay at higher altitudes, above 4,000 feet. The Carolina Chickadee, on the other hand, generally stays below this altitude. During the winter, both species will mingle at lower elevations. The differences in the song of each species can aid in distinguishing the two. The song of the Carolina chickadee is a four-noted, whistled song that sounds like *"fee-bee fee-bay"*; this is higher and faster than that of the black-capped chickadee whose two-noted song sounds like *"fee-bee."* The Carolina chickadee is 4 to 5 inches long.

The Carolina chickadee may be seen at low to middle elevations in the park including Abrams Creek, Cataloochee, Cosby, and Greenbrier Cove.

DOWNY WOODPECKER

The downy woodpecker (Picoides pubescens), which is the Smokies' smallest species of woodpecker, measures 6 to 7 inches in length. It is one of two species of woodpeckers in the park that is white-and-black checkered with a white back and belly. The other species, the hairy woodpecker (Picoides villosus), is 3 or more inches longer and has a longer bill. The male in both species has a red patch on the nape of the neck. The markings of these two woodpeckers are so similar that the downy woodpecker probably received its name because it was mistaken for an immature hairy woodpecker.

In late winter through the spring, the downy woodpecker drums on trees to establish territories and attract potential mates. The bird uses resonant surfaces, such as dead trees, for drumming or pecking in one- or two-second rapid bursts. Nests are found in hollow trees. Mated pairs will aggressively defend territories from other downy woodpeckers. The call of this woodpecker is a rapid, descending whinny of notes.

The downy woodpecker, a fairly common, permanent resident, is considered one of the most observable of North America's woodpeckers because it often approaches observers closely while foraging for food—insects that make their homes in the bark of trees. These woodpeckers may be found throughout the park, especially in the oak and cove hardwood forests below the 3,500-foot elevation. Cataloochee, Oconaluftee, Greenbrier, and Sugarlands are good places to find downy woodpeckers.

RUBY-THROATED HUMMINGBIRD

Perpetual motion, brilliant colors, and unbelievable speed are just a few of the reasons why the ruby-throated hummingbird (*Archilochus colubris*) is one of the park's most interesting wildlife species to observe. It is diminutive at 3-1/2 inches long, and its size makes it the smallest bird in the park and the only hummingbird seen regularly east of the Mississippi River.

The iridescent green body feathers are one of nature's most spectacular optical illusions. The feathers are actually a black color, but when tilted at just the right angle they reflect portions of the light spectrum creating the brilliant iridescence characteristic of hummingbirds. The male also has a red throat that the female lacks.

When displaying during the mating season, the male swings to and fro as if tied to a string. Hummingbird nests are silver-dollar-sized, composed of mosses, lichens, and spider web silk. The nest holds two small white eggs about the size of garden peas. In the Smokies, ruby-throated hummingbirds frequently build their nests over or near streams. Outside the nesting season, hummingbirds can be observed in feeding areas vying for territorial dominance by constantly chasing and harassing one another.

The ruby-throated hummingbird is most often observed feeding with its needle-like bill from the nectar of colorful, showy flowers. To find this bird, watch for flowering plants such as cardinal flower, rhododendron, and spotted touch-me-nots in bloom near moist areas of the park. Look for ruby-throated hummingbirds in Greenbrier Cove, Abrams Creek and Oconaluftee.

RED-BELLIED WOODPECKER

Upon first seeing a red-bellied woodpecker (*Melanerpes carolinus*), it is difficult to imagine why it is not called a red-headed woodpecker. If you look closely, however, you will see a reddish cast of color on the belly feathers. Also, the red-headed woodpecker's (*Melanerpes lewis*) head is entirely red, whereas the red-bellied woodpecker's red color is found only on the top of the head and nape of the neck. The red-bellied woodpecker also has black-and-white ladder striping on its back.

The robin-sized red-bellied woodpecker is most often heard communicating its territorial claims in the deciduous forests. These woodpeckers find hollow logs and trees that are selected for their resonate, sound-producing qualities and drum on them, producing the rapid hammering characteristic of woodpeckers. The drumming of the red-bellied woodpecker is softer and more rapid than the pileated woodpecker. The call of the red-bellied woodpecker uses a nasal trill to create a repetitive series of *"churr, churr, churr."*

The red-bellied woodpecker is a fairly common, permanent resident of the park; it is found at all but the highest elevations in the park. They can be seen in the forests surrounding Cade's Cove and Sugarlands.

PILEATED WOODPECKER

Flashing its broad black-and-white wings as it flies through wooded park areas, the pileated woodpecker (Dryocopus pileatus) is an impressive site. It is the largest of the park's eight species of woodpeckers and is a fairly common, permanent resident in all of the forests of the Smokies, with the exception of the spruce-fir forest.

Because it is a secretive bird, it is most often heard before it is seen. The pileated woodpecker has a high-pitched, almost jungle-like call that sounds like "kak-kak-kak." This bird drums on hollow trees to attract potential mates and help establish territories. The drumming creates a hollow, rhythmic sound that starts out loud and descends softly.

Pileated woodpeckers are crow-sized birds with an almost 2-foot wingspan. Both sexes have bright red crests and a predominantly black body. Males possess an equally bright red "mustache"; the females do not.

All woodpeckers have an interesting toe alignment called "zygodactyl." Like parrots and owls, they have two toes that point straight forward and two toes that point straight back. They also have stiff tail feathers. Both of these characteristics provide the woodpecker with the support and grip it needs to hang from a tree and feed.

These birds may be found in the lower elevations in mature hardwood forests, such as Greenbrier, Cosby, Cataloochee, and Cade's Cove.

ROSE-BREASTED GROSBEAK

The rose-breasted grosbeak (Pheucticus ludovicianus) is a part-time resident of the Great Smoky Mountains; it arrives in April and leaves for warmer climates in October. It is a starling-sized bird, about 8 inches in length. This grosbeak nests in low, woody plants, such as rhododendron, and forages for nuts and berries, such as wild cherries and sumac, in the tops of trees.

The male rose-breasted grosbeak is a handsome black-and-white bird sporting a triangular red splash of color on its chest. The female bird looks like a sparrow with the exception of its stout beak, which is used for crushing seeds and insects. The call of the grosbeak is a metallic squeak that sounds like a rusty water pump handle.

These birds may be found in the northern hardwood forest at middle elevations up to 5,000 feet. Watch for them at the edge of the forest openings as they fly from one patch of forest to another. In migration they may be seen throughout the park. During the nesting season look along the chimney tops and Acum Cave trails off the Newfound Gap Road.

SO YOU'D LIKE TO KNOW MORE?

The following list provides addresses of organizations and accommodations that you can contact for further information on your trip to the Great Smoky Mountains.

National Park Service

From mid-June through August (and less frequently in the spring and fall), park naturalists offer a number of activities at various park locations. Nature hikes and evening programs offer insight into the natural and cultural history of the Great Smoky Mountains. For more information, contact the park headquarters at 615-436-1200 or write to: Superintendent, Great Smoky Mountains National Park, Gatlinburg, TN 37738.

Spring Wildflower Pilgrimage

The three-day Spring Wildflower Pilgrimage is held the last week in April. The pilgrimage, which was instituted in 1950, has grown to include almost one hundred programs. Most of these programs emphasize the Smokies' plant life, but they also include such diverse topics as birding in the Newfound Gap, Cade's Cove, and Cosby; spider and terrestrial insect forays; salamandering to Mount Collins; and black bear walks. For more information on exact dates and program opportunities, contact the park headquarters at 615-436-1200 or write to: Superintendent, Great Smoky Mountains National Park, Gatlinburg, TN 37738.

Smoky Mountains Field School

The Smoky Mountains Field School, which is a joint effort between the University of Tennessee and the National Park Service, offers one- or two-day hikes and workshops on the park's plant and animal life. Other classes include Native American culture and the history of the park. For a nominal fee, leading experts on the Smoky Mountains lead these programs, which are geared toward adult audiences. For more information, call 1-800-284-8885 or write to Great Smoky Mountains National Park, 107 Park Headquarters Road, Gatlinburg, TN 37738.

Great Smoky Mountains Institute at Tremont

The Institute at Tremont, which is a cooperative effort between the National Park Service and the Great Smoky Mountains Natural History Association, offers two- to five-day environmental education workshops and camps for ages 9 and up. A small course fee includes meals and dormitory lodging. For more information, call 423-448-6709 or write to the Great Smoky Mountains Institute at Tremont, 9275 Tremont Road, Townsend, TN 37882.

Camping

The National Park Service operates ten developed campgrounds throughout the park. These campgrounds do not have showers or electrical hookups. Opening dates vary in each campground; Smokemont, Cade's Cove, and Elkmont are open year-round. Make reservations for these three campgrounds by calling 1-800-365-CAMP (park code, GREA). Other sites are available on a first-come first-served basis. Free permits are required for backcountry camping and are available at ranger stations and information kiosks at trailheads. There are more than 800 miles of trails found within the park, including the Appalachian Trail. Reservations may be needed for some backcountry sites. Make reservations for these sites by calling 423-436-1231. For more information on camping, contact the park headquarters.

Accommodations

LeConte Lodge, which is located on Mount LeConte, is one of the park's highest peaks at 6,593 feet and offers the only overnight lodging within the park boundaries. The lodge provides cabins and group lodges for individuals willing to hike the 5-mile trek into the heart of the park; there are no roads accessing the lodge. The lodge is a rustic retreat with meals provided in a setting far from the rush of modern society. No telephones or televisions are available. For information, call 423-429-5704 or write to LeConte Lodge, 250 Apple Valley Road, Sevierville, TN 37862.

There are no other lodging facilities within the park. For information on accommodations outside the park, contact information centers at the following nearby communities:

Bryson City, NC 1-800-867-9246

Cherokee, NC 1-800-438-1601

Fontana, NC 1-800-849-2258

Maggie Valley, NC 1-800-MAGGIE-1

Gatlinburg, TN 1-800-568-4748

Pigeon Forge, TN 1-800-251-9100

Townsend, TN 1-800-525-6834

Further Reading

The Great Smoky Mountains Natural History Association offers a free catalog of books, maps, and videos about the park. The association also operates gift shops and bookstores at Cade's Cove, Oconaluftee, and Sugarlands. The Natural History Association publishes checklists on birds, mammals, amphibians, and reptiles of the park and sponsors publication of a series of nature guides. Titles include *Birds of the Smokies* by Dr. Fred Alsop and *Trees of the Smokies* by Steve Kemp. For more information or to receive the catalog, call 423-436-0120 or write to the Great Smoky Mountains Natural History Association, 115 Park Headquarters Road, Gatlinburg, TN 37738.

Here's How to Help

The Great Smoky Mountains Natural History Association is a private, nonprofit organization formed in 1953. Its mission is to "enhance the understanding and enjoyment of the Smokies." The group sponsors informative publications, educational programs, and resource management projects. For more information, contact the Natural History Association, 115 Park Headquarters Road, Gatlinburg, TN 37738.

The Friends of Great Smoky Mountains National Park is dedicated to raising funds for the park. This group has raised funds for facility and trail development and increased educational services. For more information, call 423-453-6231 or write to the Friends of Great Smoky Mountains National Park, 134 Court Avenue, Sevierville, TN 37862.

BIBLIOGRAPHY

Alsop, Fred J. III. *Birds of the Smokies*. Great Smoky Mountains Natural History Association, 1991.

Amphibians and Reptiles of The Great Smoky Mountains. Great Smoky Mountains Natural History Association, 1993.

Behler, John L., and F. Wayne King. *National Audubon Society Field Guide to North American Reptiles and Amphibians*. Alfred A. Knopf, 1994.

Bierly, Michael L. *Bird Finding in Tennessee*. Michael Lee Bierly, 1980.

Birds of The Great Smoky Mountains. Great Smoky Mountains National Park.

Bull, John, and John Farrand, Jr. *National Audubon Society Field Guide to North American Birds, Eastern Region*. Alfred A. Knopf, 1994.

Burt, William H., and Richard Grossenheider. *A Field Guide to the Mammals: North America North of Mexico, 3rd ed.* Houghton Mifflin Company, 1980.

Carlton, Michael, and John Netherton. *Tennessee Wonders: A Pictorial Guide to the Parks*. Rutledge Hill Press, 1994.

Conant, Roger, and Joseph T. Collins. *A Field Guide to Reptiles and Amphibians: Eastern and Central North America, 3rd ed.* Houghton Mifflin Company, 1991.

Houk, Rose. *A Natural History Guide: Great Smoky Mountains National Park*. Houghton Mifflin Company, 1993.

Huheey, James E., and Arthur Stupka. *Amphibians and Reptiles of Great Smoky Mountains National Park*. The University of Tennessee Press, 1967.

Linzey, Alicia V., and Donald W. Linzey. *Mammals of Great Smoky Mountains National Park*. The University of Tennessee Press, 1971.

Mammals of The Great Smoky Mountains. Great Smoky Mountains Natural History Association, 1991.

Martin, Laura C. *Wildlife Folklore*. The Globe Pequot Press, 1994.

Peterson, Roger Tory. *A Field Guide to the Birds of Eastern and Central North America, 4th ed.* Houghton Mifflin Company, 1980.

Pyne, Milo. "Old Growth Forests in Tennessee." *Tennessee Conservationist Magazine*, December 1994.

Rezendes, Paul. *Tracking and the Art of Seeing*. Camden House Publishing, 1992.

Robbins, Chandler S., Bertel Bruun, and Herbert S. Zim. *A Guide to Field Identification: Birds of North America*. Golden Press, 1983.

Stokes, Donald. *A Guide to Bird Behavior, Vol. I*. Little, Brown and Company, 1979.

———. *A Guide to Bird Behavior, Vol. II*. Little, Brown and Company, 1985.

———. *A Guide to Bird Behavior, Vol. III*. Little, Brown and Company, 1989.

Tyning, Thomas F. *A Guide to Amphibians and Reptiles*. Little, Brown and Company, 1990.